THE MANUSCRIPT HISTORY
OF THE PSALMS OF SOLOMON

SOCIETY OF BIBLICAL LITERATURE
SEPTUAGINT AND COGNATE STUDIES SERIES

Edited by
George W. E. Nickelsburg
and
Harry M. Orlinsky

Number 13

THE MANUSCRIPT HISTORY OF THE PSALMS OF SOLOMON

by
Robert R. Hann

THE MANUSCRIPT HISTORY
OF THE PSALMS OF SOLOMON

by
Robert R. Hann

SCHOLARS PRESS

Published by
Scholars Press
101 Salem Street
P.O. Box 2268
Chico, CA 95927

THE MANUSCRIPT HISTORY
OF THE PSALMS OF SOLOMON

by
Robert R. Hann

©1982
Society of Biblical Literature

Library of Congress Cataloging in Publication Data
Hann, Robert R.
　The manuscript history of the Psalms of Solomon.
(Septuagint and cognate studies / Society of Biblical
Literature ; no. 13)(ISSN 0145-2754)
　Bibliography: p.
　Includes index.
　1. Psalms of Solomon—Criticism, Textual. I. Society of
Biblical Literature. II. Title. III. Series: Septuagint and
cognate studies ; no. 13.
BS1830.P73H36　　　229'.912048　　　　81-21212
ISBN 0-89130-557-2 (Scholars Press)　　　AACR2

Printed in the United States of America

CONTENTS

PREFACE vii

INTRODUCTION 1

CHAPTER ONE: THE STUDY OF THE *PSALMS OF SOLOMON* 3

   The Witnesses 3
   The Study of the Text to von Gebhardt 6
   The Edition of von Gebhardt 8
   The Study of the Text since von Gebhardt 10
   The Necessity for Further Study 11

CHAPTER TWO: COLLATION OF THE WITNESSES 13

CHAPTER THREE: MANUSCRIPT GROUPINGS 35

   Von Gebhardt's Stemma 35
   The Claremont Profile Method 36
   The Claremont Profile Method and the Psalms of Solomon 38
   The Manuscript Groupings 49

CHAPTER FOUR: TEXTUAL CHARACTERISTICS OF THE MANUSCRIPTS 53

   Method of Procedure 54
   The 253 Group 57
      Readings where 253 differs from 655-659 57
      Readings where 655 differs from 253-659 58
      Readings where 659 differs from 253-655 59
      Characteristics of the manuscripts of the 253 group 60
   The 260 Group 63
      The relationship of 149 to 260 63
      Readings where 149-260 differ from 471-606 64
      Readings where 471 differs from 149-260-606 . . . 65
      Readings where 606 differs from 149-260-471 . . . 66
      Readings characteristic of 3004 66
      Characteristics of the manuscripts of the 260 group 68
   The 629 group 70
      Readings where 629 differs from the majority
        of 253, 260, and 336 71
      Readings where 769 differs from the majority
        of 253, 260, and 336 71
      Characteristics of the manuscripts of the 629 group 72

CHAPTER FIVE: TEXTUAL CHARACTERISTICS OF THE TEXT TYPES . 75

   Readings of Single Groups 76
      Readings of the 253 group 76
      Readings of the 260 group 79
      Readings of 336 82
      Readings of the 629 group 86

Readings of Groups in Combination 87
  Readings of the 253 and 260 groups against
    336 and the 629 group 87
  Readings of the 253 group and 336 against
    the 260 and 629 groups 88
  Readings of the 253 and 629 groups against
    the 260 group and 336 89
Characteristics of the Text-Types 90
  Characteristics of the 253 group 91
  Characteristics of the 260 group 92
  Characteristics of 336 93
  Characteristics of the 629 group 94

CHAPTER SIX: THE MANUSCRIPT HISTORY 97

Reconstructing the Manuscript History 97
  Von Gebhardt's stemma 97
  The transmission of the text 101
Reconstructing the Text 105
  The evidence of genealogy and the documents . . . 105
  The internal evidence of readings 109
  The textual criticism of the Psalms of Solomon . . 111
Implications for Further Study 112
  The textual relationship of the Psalms of Solomon
    to other writings in the manuscripts 113
  The Syrohexaplar and the Syriac text of the
    Psalms of Solomon 113
  Geographical and historical factors in the
    manuscript tradition 114
  The textual criticism of other writings of the
    Pseudepigrapha of the Old Testament 114

NOTES 115

  Notes to Introduction 115
  Notes to Chapter One 116
  Notes to Chapter Two 123
  Notes to Chapter Three 125
  Notes to Chapter Four 130
  Notes to Chapter Five 136
  Notes to Chapter Six 142

BIBLIOGRAPHY 146

INDEX TO PASSAGES 151

  Psalms of Solomon 151
  Old Testament and Apocrypha 155
  New Testament 156

INDEX TO AUTHORS 157

PREFACE

The *Psalms of Solomon*, a collection of eighteen hymns
probably written during the first century BCE by members of a
Jewish sect in Judea, are preserved in three Syriac witnesses
and in eleven Greek MSS dating from the tenth to the sixteenth
century. Although three Greek MSS have been found since the
1895 edition of the *PsSol* by O. von Gebhardt, there has been
no thorough study of the relationships among the witnesses
since that time. The present work offers a collation of the
MSS and a detailed examination of their variant readings, and
presents a new reconstruction of the manuscript history of the
Greek text of the *PsSol*.

I wish to acknowledge the contributions of two scholars
to the present work. Dr. Robert B. Wright of Temple University
originally interested me in the *PsSol*, and produced a
provisional collation which was the initial basis of the
collation found in the second chapter of this work. Dr.
Thomas F. McDaniel of the Eastern Baptist Theological Seminary
has been a critical reader, a helpful colleague, and in many
other ways a good friend. In addition, I wish to thank
Barbara Dunevitz for her careful typing of the manuscript, a
task which involved sorting out multiple typing elements, an
unfamiliar alphabet, and innumerable handwritten corrections
between and around the lines of my first typed draft. The
errors which may be found in the present work are of course
the responsibility of its author alone.

Florida International University
Miami
31 December 1981

INTRODUCTION

Among the writings which are commonly classified together as the Pseudepigrapha of the Old Testament are the eighteen hymns of the *Psalms of Solomon*.[1] These Psalms, some of which are strongly reminiscent of the canonical Psalter in form, were produced by a group of pious Jews, probably during the first century BCE. In particular, the second, eighth, and seventeenth Psalms portray the reaction of their authors to the Roman occupation of Jerusalem in 63 BCE. These Jews understood the occupation to be the result of a general disregard for righteousness on the part of the rulers and people of Israel (17:20). They considered themselves exiles, and awaited the reign of the messiah who would redeem and purify their land (17:21-32).

Little can be said with confidence about the authorship of the *PssSol*. Scholarly consensus has described the Psalms as the product of Pharisaic circles in Jerusalem.[2] More recently, however, it has been suggested that an Essene origin may better explain the apocalyptic character of the hymns.[3] The community which produced the *PssSol* called themselves "the Pious." That their piety had resemblances to that of the Pharisees[4] and the Essenes[5] is clear; it is doubtful, however, that a certain identification of either sect as the community of origin for the *PssSol* can be made on the basis of present knowledge.[6]

It is the objective of the present work to undertake a thorough examination of the relationships among the readings of the Greek MSS of the *PssSol* and to reconstruct the genealogy of the extant witnesses. Implicit in this statement are certain qualifications. This project will not attempt to reconstruct the text of the *PssSol*, although its conclusion will discuss the implications of this study for that task. Since this work is concerned with the history of the text of these Psalms, it will not attempt to explore the historical, linguistic, theological or other background to the composition of the text. Finally, no investigation will be made of the relationship of the Greek MSS to the Syriac witnesses.

The following chapter will describe the Greek manuscripts of the *PssSol*, will outline the history of scholarship in the text of the Psalms, and will discuss the necessity for the present study. Chapter two will provide a collation of the witnesses against the text of the *PssSol* found in A. Rahlfs' *Septuaginta*.[7] Chapter three will examine the MS groupings by means of the Claremont Profile Method developed by P. R. McReynolds and F. Wisse.[8] Chapter four will investigate the characteristic readings of the component witnesses of each text group. Chapter five will examine the characteristic readings of the several text groups. Chapter six will conclude the study by reconstructing the genealogy of the textual tradition of the *PssSol*.

CHAPTER ONE
THE STUDY OF THE *PSALMS OF SOLOMON*

THE WITNESSES

The *PssSol* are preserved, in whole or in part, in eleven Greek MSS. Throughout the present work these witnesses will be cited by the numerical designations assigned to them by A. Rahlfs and his successors in the Göttingen *Septuaginta - Unternehmen*. Previous editions, including that of O. von Gebhardt, to be discussed below, designated the MSS by letters, usually the initials of the cities or libraries where they were located. The Göttingen designations are superior to the previous practice of each editor assigning his own set of designations to the witnesses, since it allows each MSS to be readily identified in all editions of each of the writings it contains.[1] The following are descriptions of the witnesses:

MS 149 (= Gebh. *V*). This MS is *Theologici Graeci* 11 of the Vienna Österreichische Nationalbibliothek. It has been dated to the eleventh century. A parchment codex of 166 folios measuring 36 x 27 cm, 149 contains *catenae* on Job and Proverbs, Ecclesiastes and Canticles with marginal commentaries, Wisdom, the *PssSol*, and Sirach. The text of the *PssSol* is contained on folios 105v - 118v.[2] The text of Wisdom and Sirach was collated in the Göttingen editions edited by J. Ziegler.[3]

MS 253 (= Gebh. *R*). This MS is *Vaticani Graeci* 336 of the Vatican library. It has been dated to the eleventh or twelfth century.[4] A parchment codex of 194 folios, 253 measures 25 x 18 cm, and contains Job, Proverbs, Ecclesiastes, Canticles, Wisdom, the *PssSol*(under the superscription Σοφια Σολομωντος), and portions of Sirach. Folios 122v - 136v contain the *PssSol*.[5] This MS was collated in the Göttingen editions of Wisdom and Sirach.[6] The superscription to Wisdom describes Wisdom, the *PssSol*, and Sirach as αδιαθετα.[7] There is evidence that 253 was once owned, perhaps in Greece by a private individual: a marginal notation in Greek, from the

3

fifteenth century, refers to the birth of the owner's brother, to his own marriage, and to the death of his mother.[8]

MS 260 (= Gebh. *K*). This MS is *Gamle Kongelige Samling* 6 of the Kongelige Bibliotek of Copenhagen. It is dated to the tenth or eleventh century. MS 260 is a parchment codex of 232 folios, and contains *catenae* on Job and Proverbs, Ecclesiastes and Canticles with marginal commentaries, Wisdom, the *PssSol*, and Sirach. The *PssSol* are found on folios 170v - 183r.[9] The text of 260 was collated in the Göttingen editions of Wisdom and Sirach.[10] The MS once belonged to Lukas Notaras, duke of Constantinople.[11] MS 260 was identified by von Gebhardt as the exemplar from which 149 is a line for line and page for page copy.[12]

MS 336 (= Gebh. *I*). This MS is number 555 of the Iberon monastery of Mt. Athos. It has been dated to the fourteenth century. A paper codex of 327 folios, 336 contains most of Job, Proverbs, Ecclesiastes, Canticles, Wisdom, Sirach, the *PssSol*, and *scholia* on Ecclesiastes, Canticles, and Proverbs.[13] There are two major lacunae in the text of the *PssSol*. The pages containing the text from the end of 5:14 through the beginning of 8:12 are missing. It appears that a leaf consisting of four sides has disappeared from the codex.[14] In addition, the text of the *PssSol* breaks off at 18:5, and is followed immediately by Sir 33:1-13.[15] The text of Wisdom and Sirach, but not of the Sirach fragment which follows the *PssSol*, has been collated in the Göttingen editions.[16]

MS 471 (= Gebh. *M*). This MS is *Bibliotheca Sanctissimae Synodi* 147 of the State Historical Museum in Moscow. It is a parchment codex dated to the twelfth to the fourteenth century.[17] The MS contains 225 folios of 35 x 27 cm. MS 471 contains *catenae* on Job and Proverbs, Ecclesiastes and Canticles with marginal commentaries, Wisdom, the *PssSol*, and Sirach. The text of the *PssSol* is contained on folios 168v - 179v. The MS originated at the Iberon monastery on Mt. Athos.[18] The text of Wisdom and Sirach was collated in the Göttingen editions.[19]

MS 606 (= Gebh. *P*). This MS is *Grec* 2991A of the Bibliothèque Nationale in Paris. The MS bears the date 1419. MS 606 is a paper codex of 495 folios of 21 x 14 cm, and contains Wisdom, the *PssSol*, and Sirach.[20] The *PssSol* appear on

Study of the Psalms 5

folios 224v - 244v. The MS was brought to Paris from Constantinople in the early eighteenth century.[21] The text of Wisdom and Sirach was collated in the Göttingen editions.[22]

MS 629 (=Gebh. *C*). This MS is number 1908 of the Biblioteca Casanatense in Rome. It has been dated to the twelfth to the fourteenth century.[23] A paper codex of 310 folios measuring 38 x 25 cm, 629 contains a *catena* on the canonical Psalms and the *Odes of Solomon* and the *PssSol*.[24] The text of the *PssSol* is found on folios 302r - 305v, and is incomplete. The text begins at 2:27 and continues to 16:8. The text following 16:8 is illegible.[25] There are in addition several other places where the text cannot be read.[26]

MS 655. This text has not been collated in previous editions of the *PssSol*. It is *Ottoboniani Graeci* 60 of the Vatican library, and has been dated to the sixteenth century. It is a paper codex of 363 folios measuring 24 x 17 cm. The text of the *PssSol* is found on folios 201r - 220r under the superscription Σοφια Σολομωντος.[27]

MS 659. This MS is similar to MS 655, and was written by the same scribe. It has not been collated in previous editions of the *PssSol*. It is *Ottobaniani Graeci* 384 of the Vatican Library, and has been dated to the sixteenth century. It is a paper codex of 354 folios of 23 x 15 cm. The *PssSol* are found on folios 208r - 226v under the superscription Σοφια Σολομωντος.[28]

MS 769 (=Gebh. *L*). This MS, which is listed in Rahlfs' *Verzeichnis der griechischen Handschriften des Alten Testaments* as number 1485 of the Laura monastery on Mt. Athos,[29] is now Codex 5 of the Benaki Museum in Athens.[30] This MS has been dated to the twelfth to the fourteenth century.[31] MS 769 is a paper codex of 311 folios measuring 28 x 19 cm. MS 769 contains a commentary on the canonical Psalms, the *Odes of Solomon* with a marginal commentary on the first ode, the *PssSol*, and a commentary on Canticles by Cyril of Alexandria. The *PssSol* are found on folios 294r - 304v.[32]

MS 3004. This fragmentary text of the *PssSol* is described in Rahlfs' *Verzeichnis* as a fragment of a commentary on the canonical psalter, and is *Vossius Miscellaneous* 15 of the Bibliotheek der Rijksuniversiteit in Leiden.[33] The MS has not been collated in previous editions of the *PssSol*. MS 3004 has been dated to the twelfth to the sixteenth century.[34] It is a paper codex measuring 22 x 16 cm and containing 83 folios. The text of the *PssSol*, which is found on folios 79r - 82v, is preceded by a lengthy commentary on Canticles.[35] The *PssSol* fragment contains the text from 17:2 to 18:12, and has been partially corrected on the basis of de la Cerda's edition.[36]

Contemporary scholarship is unanimous that the extant Greek witnesses to the *PssSol* represent a translation from an original Hebrew text.[37] An original Hebrew text of the *PssSol* is no longer extant; the psalms are preserved only in these Greek MSS and in Syriac translation.[38]

THE STUDY OF THE TEXT TO VON GEBHARDT

A detailed history of scholarship on the *PssSol* appears in J. Viteau's *Les Psaumes de Salomon*.[39] The survey which follows is a synopsis of the major items relevant to the present work, and of other studies since the publication of Viteau's edition of the *PssSol*.

The *PssSol* were circulated in the east during the early centuries of Christianity. Mentioned in several ancient lists of canonical and other sacred books,[40] these Psalms were listed on the contents page of Codex Alexandrinus and were apparently originally contained in that codex following the NT and the letters of Clement.[41] In 1884, J. Harris suggested on the basis of his analysis of the stichometry of the *PssSol* that the Psalms may also once have been contained in Codex Sinaiticus.[42]

The modern study of the *PssSol* began in the early seventeenth century, with the discovery of the Psalms by D. Hoeschel, the librarian of Augsburg, in a MS which contained other Solomonic materials. Hoeschel intended to publish the text of the *PssSol*, but died in 1617 before this could be accomplished.[43]

The text of the Psalms was published, together with a Latin translation, by J. L. de la Cerda in 1626, as an appendix to his massive *Adversaria Sacra*.[44] De la Cerda edited the *PssSol* on the basis of a text which he had received from his fellow Jesuit A. Schott, who had known of Hoeschel's discovery.[45] The text which Schott sent to de la Cerda was long believed to have been

Study of the Psalms   7

a copy or the MS itself[46] of a now-lost Codex Augustanus.[47] In
1895 von Gebhardt demonstrated that this supposed Augsburg codex
was in reality MS 149 of Vienna, from which a defective copy
had been made and sent to de la Cerda.[48] De la Cerda was aware
of the poor quality of his exemplar and suggested several emendations in his notes.[49]

The next edition of the *PssSol* was by J. A. Fabricius in
1713. Fabricius reproduced de la Cerda's text, and introduced
several conjectural emendations.[50] He was the first editor to
take notice of MS 149 in the Vienna library.[51]

In 1869 Hilgenfeld published the text of the *PssSol* in
his *Messias Judaeorum*.[52] His text was based on de la Cerda's
edition, and included in the collation readings of 149 and
Fabricius.[53] He included in addition his own conjectures and
those of P. de Lagarde.[54] Hilgenfeld believed that the Psalms
were originally written in Greek.[55]

In 1871 E. E. Geiger published a Greek text of the *PssSol*
with a German translation.[56]

In 1981 O. F. Fritzsche published the text of the Psalms
in his *Libri Apocryphi Veteris Testamenti Graece*.[57] His collation included readings from 149, de la Cerda, Fabricius, and
Hilgenfeld.[58] He believed that the Psalms were composed in
Hebrew after the death of Pompey.[59]

In 1974 J. Wellhausen published a German translation of
the *PssSol* with notes, as an appendix to his *Die Pharisäer und
die Sadducäer*.[60] His notes included conjectural emendations of
the text, several of which were based on his reconstruction of
the original Hebrew archetype.[61]

The first English translation of the *PssSol* was that of
B. Pick in 1883.[62] Pick included the Greek and English texts in
parallel columns, and made use of 149, de la Cerda, Fabricius,
and Hilgenfeld.[63]

The first major step beyond the work of Hilgenfeld was the
edition of the *PssSol* of Ryle and James in 1891.[64] In addition
to using 149 and de la Cerda, Ryle and James made use of 260 of
Copenhagen, 471 of Moscow, and 606 of Paris.[65] By comparing the
extent of agreement among these witnesses, the editors constructed a genealogical stemma in which 149 and de la Cerda were
related in a group contrasting with the group 260-471-606.[66]

Ryle and James believed that the Psalms were composed in Hebrew,[67] and provided notes on the nature of the translation into Greek.[68] The editors included the suggestion that the present eighteenth Psalm may originally have been composed as two separate Psalms.[69] This conjecture received support from the later discovery that MS 3004 divides *PsSol* 18 along the lines that Ryle and James had suggested.[70]

In 1894 a portion of textual evidence in addition to that used by Ryle and James was utilized in the Greek text published by H. B. Swete in the third volume of his *The Old Testament in Greek According to the Septuagint*.[71] In addition to 149, 260, 471, and 606, which had appeared in Ryle and James' edition, Swete collated MS 253 from the Vatican library. His collation makes little use of conjectural emendation.[72] Swete's text of the *PsSol* was issued in a second edition in 1899, which collated the additional MS evidence of 336, 629, and 769.[73]

THE EDITION OF VON GEBHARDT

The most thorough edition of the Greek text of the *PsSol* is the 1895 work by von Gebhardt, *Die Psalmen Salomo's*.[74] An important contribution by von Gebhardt was his identification of 149 as the text of which a copy was used by de la Cerda. As recently as the edition of Ryle and James in 1891, it was believed that the text of de la Cerda's edition was based on an old parchment MS of the Augsburg library.[75] Ryle and James had considered the theory that the text of de la Cerda and MS 260 might be the same, but rejected the possibility on the basis of the disagreements which they noted between the two texts.[76]

Von Gebhardt noted that all attempts to locate the Augsburg codex were unsuccessful. He rejected the possibility that the MS itself might have been sent to de la Cerda, on the assumption that the latter had need of only a few pages, and since de la Cerda's expressions "in Greek" and "it is written" imply that he was not thereby referring to the codex itself.[77] Furthermore, the only informant that there was at Augsburg a codex containing the *PsSol* was de la Cerda himself, who received the information from his correspondent A. Schott. In Schott's letter to J. Meursius, however, dated October 23, 1614,

Study of the Psalms   9

it was only stated that Hoeschel had an old MS from Constantinople which contained Salomonic writings. This language could have been used if Hoeschel had borrowed a MS from another library or had received a copy from a friend. One of Hoeschel's correspondents was S. Tengnagel, the librarian of Vienna. Since Fabricius had noted less than a century earlier that a MS containing the *PssSol* existed in Vienna, the possibility existed that MS 149, the Vienna codex, was the source of the text used by Hoeschel and from which a copy was sent to de la Cerda.[78] This possibility was confirmed in a letter to von Gebhardt from A. G. von Tiefenau of the Vienna library, who wrote that the Vienna codex was actually sent to Hoeschel, and that chapter numbers for Sirach now appear in the codex in Hoeschel's handwriting.[79] Von Gebhardt concluded: "Die Editio princeps mit ihrem Ballast von schlechten Lesarten ist also aus der Reihe der Textzeugen zu streichen."[80]

A second major contribution by von Gebhardt was his refinement of the relationship among the MSS which were known at that time. In addition to the witnesses which were used in Swete's 1894 edition, von Gebhardt utilized 336, 629, and 769.[81] Of the eight MSS which he analyzed, 149, 260, 471, and 606 were identified, on the basis of comparing their readings, as forming a distinct text group.[82] The closest relationship is between 149 and 260, which are virtually identical line for line.[83] Von Gebhardt concluded that 260 is the earliest of these MSS on the basis of a minute examination of the text at 16:13, where the scribe of 260 made a correction of his own error, a correction which was misread by the copyists of 149 and the other witnesses of the text group.[84] Von Gebhardt believed that 253 most reliably preserves the common archetype of the remaining MSS, since that witness has preserved grammatical features characteristic of the oldest biblical MSS.[85] The relationship among the remaining MSS was determined by comparing their readings. This comparison showed that 336 stands closest to 253 and that the text behind 629 and 769 stands between 336 and 260.[86] MSS 629 and 769 stem from a common ancestral text.[87] From these conclusions, von Gebhardt produced a stemma which has been adopted by subsequent scholarship.[88] Von Gebhardt's

collation does not include all of the readings of these eight
MSS. The readings of 260 were used to represent the group 149-
260-471-606.[89]

THE STUDY OF THE TEXT SINCE VON GEBHARDT

In 1899 Swete published a second edition of his text of
the *PssSol*, including in his collation the witnesses which had
been examined by von Gebhardt. This edition collated all eight
MSS throughout and is the most complete published collation of
the *PssSol* to date.[90]

In 1909 J. R. Harris published a Syriac text of the *PssSol*
based on a single MS.[91] Harris concluded that the Syriac is a
translation of the Greek version of the Psalms.[92] In 1916
Harris, together with Alphonse Mingana, published an edition of
the Syriac text which was based on three MSS.[93]

In 1911 J. Viteau published an edition of the *PssSol* with
an introduction, the Greek text, and a French translation.[94]
As has been noted above, his introduction provides a valuable
summary of previous scholarship.

In 1913 G. B. Gray published an introduction to the
PssSol with an English translation and critical notes in Charles'
APOT.[95] This is the most recently published English translation
of the Psalms.

In 1937 K. G. Kuhn published *Die älteste Textgestalt der
Psalmen Salomos*. Kuhn contended that the Syriac version of the
PssSol is an immediate translation from Hebrew, and is not de-
pendent on a Greek text.[96]

In 1939 J. Begrich published "Der Text der Psalmen
Salomos," in which he reasserted the dependence of the Syriac
version on the Greek. A major contribution of Begrich's work
was his comparison of the readings of the Greek and Syriac MSS,
in which he concluded that the Syriac and MS 253 stem from a
common textual ancestor.[97]

In 1955 W. Pesch published a study of the relationship of
PsSol 11 to Bar 5, concluding that the author of the Psalm made
use of exilic themes found in Bar 5.[98]

In 1961 W. Baars published a collation of *PsSol* 17:2-18:12
contained in MS 3004.[99]

Study of the Psalms   11

In 1965 M. de Jonge published a study of the eschatology of the *PsSol*. Included in this work are several notes on variant readings in the *PsSol*.[100]

In 1975 R. Wright and R. Hann published a critical note on the fragment of Sirach which follows *PsSol* 18:5 in MS 336.[101]

In 1976 Wright circulated privately a provisional collation of the *PsSol* which incorporated readings of all the MSS known to date.[102]

THE NECESSITY FOR FURTHER STUDY

There can be no reason to dissent from de Jonge's statement that the best edition of the *PsSol* to date is that of von Gebhardt.[103] With the single exception that Swete's 1899 edition of the Psalms included a more complete collation of the witnesses, von Gebhardt's study remains the most important treatment of the *PsSol* to date, and is that from which any subsequent examination of the text of the Psalms must begin. There remain, however, several reasons why a new examination of the Greek text of the *PsSol* is necessary.

Since 1895 new textual evidence has been discovered. MSS 655 and 659 were described in Rahlfs' *Verzeichnis* of 1914, and 3004 was collated by W. Baars in 1961.[104] The readings of these witnesses have not been collated in any edition of the *PsSol*, nor has the relationship between these MSS and the other witnesses been critically examined.

Another development which requires a new examination of the Greek text of the *PsSol* is the availability of photographic copies of the MSS. Of the eight witnesses used by von Gebhardt, only 149, 253, 471, and 606 had been examined by von Gebhardt himself.[105] In his work on 260, 336, 629, and 769 he was dependent on collations made by others.[106] In addition, von Gebhardt was limited to the use of collations even when he had direct access to the MSS: there was no other way by which he could compare the readings of MSS from different libraries. The collations of 471 and 606 were made three years apart.[107] The availability of photographs of the MSS allows a direct access and a comparison of their readings in a way which was not possible to von Gebhardt.

A final reason for a new examination of the text of the
PsSol is the limited scope of von Gebhardt's work. Although
he had access to eight witnesses and made use of all eight in
his study, his apparatus regularly includes readings only from
253, 260, 336, 629, and 769. Von Gebhardt used the readings of
260, which he believed to be the ancestor of 149, 471, and 606,
to represent the texts of these MSS.[108] Variant readings from
these MSS appear only occasionally in the apparatus, and instances where they depart from 260 are not always recorded.[109]

The following chapter will provide a collation of the
readings of the MSS against the text found in Rahlfs' *Septuaginta*.

CHAPTER TWO

COLLATION OF THE WITNESSES

Among the decisions which must be made before a collation can be constructed are the following: which witnesses are to be collated, which kinds of variant readings are to be included, and against which base text is the collation to be made.[1]

The most important edition of the *PssSol* is that of O. von Gebhardt in 1895 who, as has been seen above, did not collate all the MSS which were known at that time.[2] Von Gebhardt collated only 253, 260, 336, 629, and 769. MS 260, the archetypal member of the group 149-260-471-606, was used to represent the text of that group. Readings of other MSS of the group, most often 471, appear infrequently in his apparatus.[3] Von Gebhardt's collation included the superscriptions to the individual Psalms and variations in punctuation, accent, and breathing. His collation was made against his own reconstruction of the probable original text of the *PssSol*.[4] Von Gebhardt's text is the basis of the *PssSol* text found in Rahlfs' *Septuaginta*.[5]

In 1976 R. Wright circulated privately a collation of the *PssSol* entitled *The Psalms of Solomon: a Provisional Collated Greek Text*.[6] In addition to the MSS collated by von Gebhardt, Wright included 149, 471, and 606, the newer MSS 655, 659, and 3004, and the text of de la Cerda.[7] Wright's collation included the superscriptions to the Psalms but did not regularly include variations involving breathing, accent, punctuation, or word division. Wright's collation was against an eclectic base of his own construction.

The collation which appears on the following pages represents a thorough revision of Wright's provisional work. Wright's collation has been checked against the photographic copies of the MSS, and over 375 alterations have been made. Use has been made of a collation of MSS 655 and 659 by J. Beck.[8]

Readings from de la Cerda's edition do not appear in this collation. Since von Gebhardt has demonstrated that de la Cerda's text was based on a faulty copy of 149, nothing can be learned about the textual tradition of the *PssSol* by including these readings.[9]

14   Psalms of Solomon

I have followed Wright in omitting from this collation
variants involving breathing, accent, punctuation, or word
division, since these variations often reflect scribal idiosyn-
crasies and do not provide information about the history of the
text.[10] The superscriptions to the individual psalms have also
been omitted from consideration. Variant readings in the superscriptions are often the result of spelling and other scribal
changes. Furthermore, any apparent significance to the manuscript relationships in the superscriptions could only be proven
to be so by being confirmed by the patterns of relationships
which are found in the text itself.[11]

This collation has been made against the base of the text
of the PssSol which is found in Rahlfs' Septuaginta. This text,
which is based on von Gebhardt's work, has been chosen as the
collation base since it is the most readily accessible Greek
text of the PssSol.

I have adopted the following sigla for use in the collation below:

-       The MSS named omit this reading
+   The MSS named add this reading
*   The original reading of a corrected MS
c   The corrected reading of a MS
pr   Precedes the first word which Rahlfs prints
        of that verse

The present work follows established practice in omitting
accents and breathing marks from the apparatus.[12]

THE COLLATION

1:1	Εβοησα	βοησα 471
	του	- 253 655 659
1:2	ειπα	- all witnesses
	επακουσεται	επακουσεσε 655*
	επλησθην	επλησθη 655 659
	δικαιοσυνης	δικαιοσσυνης 769
1:3	επλησθην	επλησθη 655 659
	ευθηνησαι	ευθυνησαι 655 659
	πολλην	πολυν 149 260 336 471 606
	γενεσθαι	γηνεσθαι 655*
		γηενεσθαι 655c 659*
		γεινεσθαι 659c
1:4	διεδοθη	διελθοι 149 260 471 606 655 659
	η	η η 769
	αυτων	αυτου 769
	εσχατου	+ την γην και η δοξα αυτων εως εσχατου 253

Collation   15

1:5	εως	- 655 659
	ειπαν	ειπον 769
	πεσωσιν	πεσωσι 336 471 606
		πεσωσι μεν 769
1:7	και εγω	καγω 149 260 471 606 655 659
	ηδειν	ηδου 655*
2:1	εν	ν 471
	κατεβαλε	κατεβαλλε 253 336
		καταλλε 655
		καταβαλλε 659
2:2	κατεπατουσαν	κατεπατουν 149 260 336 471 606 769
		καταπατουσαν 655 659
	υποδημασιν	υπο ποδημασιν 655 659
2:3	εβηβλουσαν	εβηβλουν 149 260 336 471 606 769
2:4	απορριφατε	απoριψατε 253 655 659
		απερριφατε 336
	απ'	απο 655 659
	ευδοκω εν	ευωδωκεν 149 260 471 606
		ευοδωκεν 253 336 769
		ενεδωκεν εν τουτων ειπεν 655* 659*
2:5	αυτης	αυτου 149 253 260 336 606 655 659 769
	εξουθενωθη	εξουθενηθη 149 260 471 606
	ητιμωθη	επιμωττη 655 659
	εως	- 149 260 471 606
2:6	οι	- 253 655 659
	αι	- 253 655 659
	εθνεσιν	εθνεσι 149 260 471 606
2:7	κατα	ατα 471
	εγκατελιπεν	εγκατελειπεν 253
		ενκατελειπεν 655 659
	κατισχυοντων	κατεσχυοντων 655 659
		κτισχυοντων 769
2:8	απεστρεψεν	απεστρεψε 149 260 336 471 606
	το	- 149 260 336 471 606 769
	ελεους	ελεου 149 260 336 471 606 769
	αυτων	αυτου 336
	πρεσβυτην	πρεσβητην 655
		πρεστβυτην 659
	ακουειν	ακουον 655 659
2:9	εβαρυθυμησεν	εβαρυθυμησε 149 253 260 471 606
		εβαρυθμησε 655 659
	εβδελυξατο	βδελυξατο 655 659
	εποιησε	εποιησεν 659
2:10	τα (1)	ται 655 659
	παντα τα δικαια	τα δικαια παντα 336
2:11	εστησαν	εστησεν 149 260
		στησε 471
		εστησε 606
	εμπαιγμον	εμπεγμον 253
		εμπαγμον 655 659
	παραπορευομενος	πορευομενος 253 655 659
2:12	ενεπαιζον	ενεπεζον 655 659
	ταις	τας 655 659
	ανομιαις	ανομιας 655 659
2:13	θυγατερες	θυγατερας 655 659
	εμιαιωσαν	εμιαινον 149 260 336 471 606 769
	αυτας	εαυτας 149 260 336 471 606 769
	αναμειξεως	αναμιξεως all witnesses
2:14	σπλαγχνα	σπλαχνα 336 769

16   Psalms of Solomon

2:15	εγω	γω 471
	κριμασιν	κριμασι 149 260 336 471 606 769
2:16	και	- 149 260 336 471 606 769
	σφοδρα	σφοδρον 253
		σφοδραν 655 659
2:17	ανεκαλυψας	ενεμψας 655
		εκαμψας 659
	εξηλειψας	εξηλιψας 253 655 659*
		εξηυλιψας 659c
2:18	ο	- 471
	θαυμασει	θαυμασε 655 659
2:19	ωνειδισαν	ωνιδησαν 253 655 659
		ονειδισαν 336
		ωνειδισας 471
	εν καταπατησει	καταπατησαι 336
	κατεσπασθη	κατεσπασε 149 260 336 471 606 769
		κατεσπασεν 253
		κατεπαια 655
		κατεπαισεν 659
2:21	περιειλατο	περιειλετο 149 260 336 471 606 655 659 769
	μιτραν	μητραν 336 769
	απερριφη	απερριφει 253 655 659
2:22	κυριου	+ του θεου 336
	και (3)	καγω 336
	κυριε	- 336
	του βαρυνεσθαι χειρα σου	
		χειρα σου του βαρυνεσθαι 336
	χειρα	χειρας 253 655 659
	Ιερουσαλημ	Ισραηλ 253
	εν	- 655 659
	επαγωγη	απαγωγη 149 260
2:23	ενεπαιξαν	ενεπαιζαν 253 655 659
	μηνισεως	μηνησεως 149 260 471 606
	συντελεσθησονται	συντελσθσονται 471
	επιτιμησης	επιτιμησεις 253 655 659
	αυτοις	αυτους 336 769
2:24	ζηλει	ζηλω 149 260 336 471 606 769
	αλλ'	αλλα 471 659
		αλλλ 655
	εκχεαι	εκχεας 336
		εκχαιε 655 659
2:25	μη	pr και 253 655 659
	χρονισης	χρονησης 253
		λεγονησεις 655 659
	ατιμια	αιτιαμια 253 655 659
		ατιμιαμια 336
2:26	εχρονισα	εχρονησα 253 655 659
	εως	+ ου 336
	εδειξεν	εδειξε 149 260 336 471 606
		εδωξε 655 659
	ελαχιστον	ελαχιστου all witnesses
2:27	διαφερομενου	διεφαρμενου 149 260 471 606
	ο θαπτον	629 text begins[13]
	εξουθενωσεν	εξουδενωσεν 149 260 336 471 606 769
2:28	εστιν	εστι 149 260 471 606 629
2:29	ειπεν	ειπειν 769
		629 illegible
	μεγας	+ και or κυριος 629
		+ και 471

Collation

	ισχυι	ισχυει 253 655 659
2:31	ο	- 149 260 336 471 606
	απωλειαν	απωλιαν 253
		απολιαν 655 659
	αιωνος	αιωνιον 149 260 336 471 606 629 769
	ατιμια	ατομια 655 659
	αυτον	αυτων 769
2:32	του	- 149 260 336 471 606 629 769
	κρινων	κρονον 336 769
2:33	επιστημη	επιστημι 253
	κυριου	αυτου 629* 769
	αυτον	αυτου 655 659
2:34	μεσον	μεσων 253 655 659
2:35	ελεησαι	ελεησας 655 659
	ταπεινωσεως	ταπηνωσεως 655 659
	αμαρτωλου	+ αποδυναι αμαρτωλοις εις τον αιωνα κατα τα εργα αυτων 336
	εποιησεν	εποιησε 149 260 336 471 606 629
2:36	υπομονη	υπομονης 769
	ποιησαι	ποιησας 655 659
	οσιοις	μετ' 149 260 471 606 629
	παρεσταναι	παρασταναι 336
	ισχυι	ισχυει 253 336 655 659
3:1	καινον	και αινον 253 629 655 659 769
	ψαλατε	ψαλλετε 253 655 659
		ψαλλατε 471
3:2	ψαλλε και	ψαλαι 336
	θεω	κυριω 336
	αγαθης	ολης 149 260 471 606 629 769
3:3	μνημονευουσιν	μνημονευουσι 149 260 336 471 606 620 769
	κριματα	+ του 253 655 659
3:4	ολιγωρησει	ολιγορησει 253 655 659
	υπο	+ του 253 655 659
	εναντι	εναντιον 149 260 336 471 606 629 769
3:5	προσεκοψεν	προσεκιψεν 655 659
	εδικαιωσεν	εδικαιωσε 149 260 336 471 606 629 769
		εδικαιοσεν 655 659
	επεσεν	επεσε 149 260 336 471 606 629
	αποσκοπευσει	αποσκοπευε 655 659
	ηξει	+ η 336 606
	αυτου	αυτω 253 629* 655 659
3:6	αληθεια	αληθια 253 655 659
	αυλιζεται	ευλιζεται 655 659
	οικω	+ του 149 260 336 471 606 769
3:8	εξιλασατο	εξηλασατο 655 659
	ψυχης	ψυχην all witnesses
	αυτου (1)	- 253 655 659
	παν	παντα 149 260 336 471 606 629 769
	οσιον	θειον 629 769
3:9	προσεκοψεν	+ ο 336
	καταραται	+ την 336
	ζωην	ζωης 655 659
3:10	προσεθεκεν	προσεθεκαν 149 260 471 606
		629 illegible
	αμαρτιας	αμαρτιαις 253 629 655 659 769
	πτωμα	σπερμα 336
	αναστησεται	ανεστησεται 655*
		ανυστησεται 655c
3:11	ου	+ μη 253 655 659

18   Psalms of Solomon

	μνησθησεται	μνυσθησεται 655 659
	επισκεπτηται	επισκεπτεται 336
		επισκοπτηται 655 659
3:12	η (1)	- 149 260 336 471 606 629 769
	τον (2)	- 149 260 471 606 629 769
	αιωνιον	αιωνιος 336
	και (2)	- 253 655 659
		αι 336
	εκλειψει	εκλειψη 253 655 659
4:1	βεβηλε, καθησαι	καθησαι βεβηλε 149 260 336 606 629
		καθησε βεβηλε 769
	οσιων	- 149 260 471 606
		οσιω 253 655 659
	του	- 336
4:2	σημειωσει	σειμειωσει 655 659*
	ο	- 336
		οι 655 659
	κατακριναι	κατακρινων 149 260 471 606
		κατακρινει 629 769
		καταρινας 655
		κατακρινας 659
4:3	πρωτοις	η ρωτοις 655* 659*
	αυτον	αιτιον 471¹⁴
	ζηλει	ζηλω 149 260 336 471 606 629 769
	αμαρτιων	αμαρτωλων 253 655 659
	και (3)	- 253 655 659
4:4	αυτου (2)	- 253 655 659
	συναλλαγματι	συναλαγματι 659
4:5	ως	ς 655*
	ουχ	οχ' 253 655 659
	παση	πασα 659*
	εισοδω	εισωδω 655 659
	οικιαν	οικειαν 253
	εν (5)	- 253 655 659
	ιλαροτητι	ιλαροτι 253 655 659
	ακακος	ακκος 253 655 659
4:6	πενια	πενα 655*
		πολεμα 655c 659
4:7	ανακαλυψαι	ανακαλυψασας 655*
		ανακαλυψασαι 655c
4:8	δικαιωσαισαν	δικαιωσαιεν 149 260 471 606 769
		δικαιωσαιαν 629
		δικαιωσασαν 655*
		+ οι 149 260 336 471 606
	προσωπου	+ του 336
	νομον	μονον 253 655 659
	δολου	δουλου 253 655 659
4:9	αυτων	αυτου 336
	επ' οικον	εν οικω 149 260 471 606
	ευσταθεια	ευσταθια 253 336 471 606 655 659
4:10	αδικου	αδικων 253 655 659
	απεστη	ανεστη 149 260 471 606
	ενικησεν	ενικησε 149 260 336 471 606
		629 illegible
4:11	οικον	- 149 260 471 606
		629 illegible
4:12	ολεθρευσαι	ολοθρευσαι 149 260 336 471 606 629 769
4:13	εμπιπλαται	εμπελαται 659
		εμπιμπλαται 769

Collation   19

	αυτον	+ ο 336
	ως αδης	- 149 260 471 606
4:15	οδυναις	οδωναις 655
	και (1)	+ εν 149 260 471 606
	και (2)	- 253 655 659
	λυπαις	οδυναις 149 260 471 606
	εξεγερσις	εγερσις 336
	αποριαις	απορια 471 606
		απoριας 659
4:16	αφαιρεθειη	αφαιρευθιη 655
		αφαιρευθειη 659
	αποπεσοι	αποπεσοιεν 253
		αποπεσει 471 606
		αποπασοιεν 655 659
	χειρων	χειρος 471 606
		χειρως 655 659
	εν ατιμια	- 253 655 659
4:17	κενος κερσιν αυτου εισελθοι εις τον οικον αυτου
		- 253 655 659
	ελλιπης	ελλειπης 253 655 659 769
4:18	μονωσει	μονια 253 655 659
	αναλημψιν	αναληψιν 149 260 336 471 606 629 655 659 769
4:19	σκορπισθεισαν	pr ου 655 659
4:20	οφθαλμους εκκοφαισαν κορακες
		εκκοψειαν κορακες οφθαλμους ανθρωπων
		149 260 336 471 606 629 769
	υποκρινομενων	υποκρινιμενων 655 659
	ηρημωσαν	ηρημωσεν 253 655 659
	πολλους ανθρωπων	ανθρωπων πολλων 629 769
	εσκορπισαν	εσκορπισεν 253 655 659
	εν (2)	- 253 655 659
4:21	ουκ εφοβηθησαν	ου και φοβηθησαν 769
	θεον (1)	κυριον 655 659
	απασι	πασι 149 260 336 471 606
	παρωργισαν	παροργησαν 253 655 659
	παρωξυναν	παρωξυνεν 253
		παρωξηνεν 655 659
4:22	εξαραι	εξαρας 655 659
	υπεκρινοντο	υπεκρυνοντο 336
		υπεκρινετο 659
4:23	αυτων	+ και 253 655 659
	ρυσεται (2)	ρησεται 655
	ημας	υμας 655 659
4:24	εξαραι	ξαραι 655 659
	υπερηφανια	υπεριφανια 655 659
5:1	αινεσω	εναισω 655 659
	τω ονοματι	το ονομα 336 471 606
5:2	συ χρηστος	ευχρηστος 253 655 659
	η	ει 149 260 471 606
	παρασιωπησης	παρασιωπησεις 659
5:3	ου γαρ	ουτας 655 659
	ου γαρ ληψεται τις σκυλα παρα ανδρος δυνατου
		- 629 769
	τις	- all witnesses
	σκυλα	+ ανθρωπος 149 260 471 606
	παρα	απο 336
		- 471
5:4	σου	σοι 149 260 471 606
5:5	σε	- 253 655
		και 659

20 Psalms of Solomon

	αποστρεψη	αποστρεψεις 149 260 471 606
		αποστρεψης 336
		629 illegible
	οτι συ ο θεος ημων	
		- 655 659
	ει	tr post συ 149 260 336 471 606 629 769
5:6	βαρυνης	βαρυνεις 336
	δι'	δ' 655 659
5:7	αφεξομευα	αφεσομεθα 655 659
	αλλ'	αλλα 149 260
5:8	πεινασω	πινασω 253 336 655 659
	συ	σοι 336
5:9	τρεφεις	+ κυριε 629[15]
	υετον	+ εν 149 260 336 471 606 629 769
		εις τον 655 659
5:10	ητοιμασας	ετοιμασαι all witnesses
	χορτασματα	χορασματα 655 659
	ερημω	ερημιω 655 659
	πεινασωσιν	πεινασωσι 149 260 336 471 606
		πινασωσιν 253 655 659
		πεινησωσι 629 769
	αρουσιν	αρουσι 149 260 471 606 629 769
	προσωπον	προσωπα 149 260 471 606 629 769
5:11	και (1)	+ τους 149 260 471 606
	τρεφεις	στρεφεις 253
		στεφεις 655 659
	ελπις	ελπης 655 659
5:12	επακουση	επακουσης 253 655 659
	ευφραναι	+ και 149 260 336 471 606
	ελεει	ελεω 149 260 336 471 606 629
		ελεη 655 659
		ελαιω 769
5:13	φειδοι	φιλω 149 260 471 606
		φειδω 253 629 655 659 769
	και εαν	και εαν και 149 260 336 471 606
	δευτερωση	δευτερωσει 655 659
	θαυμασειας	θαυμασιασω 629 769
		θαυμασας 655 659
5:14	χρηστοτητος	+ τελος 336 margin
		omit following text to 8:12 336
	ου εστιν	ουκ εστιν 253
		ουκ εστη 655 659
	η ελπις επι σε	επι σε κυριε η ελπις 149 260 471 606 629 769
	εν	εαν 655 659
5:16	αυταρκειας	αυταρκεσιας 149 260 471 606
		αυταρκιας 253 655 659
5:17	πλησμονην	πλεισμονην 253
5:18	ευφρανθειησαν	ευφρανθησαν 149 260 471 606 629 769
		πυφρανθησαν 253 655 659
	εν (2)	- 253 655 659
5:19	ευλογημενη	ευλογιμενη 655 659 769
	βασιλευς	βασειλευς 629
6:1	επικαλεσασθαι	επικαλεισθαι 149 260 471 606
	μνημονευειν	μνημονευεσθαι 655
		μνημονευεν 659
6:3	οπασεως	ορασεων 149 260 471 606 629 769
	πονηρων	πονηρον 659*
	διαβασει	διαβασετε 655 659

Collation   21

	σαλω	σαλων 149 260 336 471 606
		σαλον 253 629 655 659 769
	πτοηθησεται	πτωηθησεται 253
6:4	ηυλογησεν	ευλογησε 149 260 471 606 629
		ευλογησεν 655 659
	τω ονοματι (1)	το ονομα 149 260 471 606
	κυριου επ' ευσταθεια καρδιας αυτου εξυμνησεν τω ονοματι
		- 655 659
	ευσταθεια	ευσταθια 253 471 606
	εξυμνησεν	εξυμνησε 149 260 471 606 629
	τω ονοματι (2)	το ονομα 149 260 471 606
	αυτου (3)	- 253 655 659
6:5	κυριος	- 655 659
	εισηκουσε	εισηκουσεν 149 260 471 606 629 769
6:6	ο (1)	- 149 260 471 606 629 769
	ελεος	ελεον 149 260 606
7:1	επιθωνται	απιθωνται 655* 659
	ημιν	ημη 655 659
	εμισησαν	μισησαντες λ49 260 471 606 629 769
7:2	πατησατο	πατισατο 253
	αγιασματος	αγαιασματος 769
7:3	θεληματι	εθεληματι 655 659
	εθνεσιν	εθνεαν 655 659
7:4	γαρ	- 655 659
	αποστειλης	αποστελης 655 659
7:6	εν	ν 471
7:7	συ	- 629 769
	επακουση	επακουσεις 629 769
7:8	οικτιρησεις	οικτειρησεις 149 253 260 471 606 629
		οικτηρμων 655*
		οικτηρησας 655c 659
		οικτηρησεις 769
	απωση	απωσει 253
		αποσει 655 659
7:9	παιδειας	παιδιας 253
		παιδιασε 655 659
		παιδεια 769
		629 illegible
7:10	η	ω 253 655 659
	επηγγειλω	επειγγειλω 769*
8:1	θλιψιν	λιψιν 471
	ηκουσεν	ηκουσε 149 260 471 606 629 769
	το ους	η ψυχη 629
	ολεθρον	+ ψυχην σαλπιγγος ηκουσης σφαγην και ολεθρον 769
8:2	φωνη	φωνην 655 659
	σφοδρα ως καταιγις πυρος πολλου
		- 655 659
	πολλου (2)	+ ως ανεμου πολλου 629 769
8:3	ειπα	ειπον 149 260 471 606 629 769
	εν	- all witnesses
	κρινει	κρονει 655 659
	αυτον	αυτην 629 769
8:4	εις	εν 149 260 471 606
8:6	ειπα	ειπον 149 260 471 606 629 769
		ειτα 655 659
	κατευθυνουσιν	ατευθυνουσιν 471
	οδους	δους 253 655 659
	αυτων	αυτον 655 659
8:7	ανελογισαμην	αναλογησαμην 253

22   Psalms of Solomon

	κτισεως	κρισεως 655 659
	εδικαιωσα	εδικαιωσαν 655 659
8:8	ανεκαλυψεν	ανακαλυψεν 253 659
		ανακαληψεν 655
	εναντιον	εναντιων 629 769
	εγνω	εγνωσαν 629 769
8:9	εν	εις 655 659
	καταγαιοις	καταγαιης 769
	κρυφιοις	κρυφοις 629 769
	θυγατρος	θυτρος 629 769
8:10	εμοιχωντο	μοιχωντο 471
	την	- 149 260 471 606 629 769
	συνεθεντο	συνενθεντο 769
8:11	διηρπαζοσαν	διηρπαζον 149 260 471 606 629 769
		διηρπαζωσαν 253
	ως μη	ουκ 149 260 471 606 629 769
8:12	επατουσαν	επατουν 149 260 471 606 629 769
	θυσιαστηριον	θυσιηστηριον 629
		θυσιαιτηριον 769
	και	text resumes 336
	αφεδρω	αφαιδρω 471
		αφαιδρων 655 659
		+ δι' 655 659
	εμιαναν	εμιαινον 149 260 336 471 606 629 769
8:13	παρελιπον	παρελειπον 253 655 659
8:14	εκερασεν	εκερασαν 655 659
	αυτους	αυτοις 149 260 606
8:15	ηγαγεν	ηγαγε 149 260 336 471 606 629
	τον (1)	το 655 659
	εσχατου	αισχατου 253 336 655 659
	της	ης 471
	τον (2)	- 336
	εκρινεν	εκρινε 149 260 336 471 606 629 769
8:16	απηντησαν	ηπυντησαν 253
		ετπατησαν 655
		επατησαν 659
	ειπαν	ειπον 149 260 336 606 769
		629 illegible
	εισελθατε	εισελθετε 149 260 336 471 606 629
8:17	ωμαλισαν	ομαλισαν 336
	τραχειας	ταραχει 655
		ταραχειας 659
	αυτου	αυτων 149 260 471 606
		629 illegible
	τευχη	τοιχη 655
8:18	εις	ις 471
	υιων	υιω 655 659
	εστησεν	εστησε 149 260 336 471 606 629
8:19	πυργοβαρεις	πυργοβαστας 655 659
	ο	- 149 260 336 471 606 629 769
	πλανησει	πλανη 655 659
8:20	απωλεσεν	εκαλεσεν 655 659
	παν	παντα 140 260 336 471 606 629 769
	εξεχεεν	εξεχεε 149 260 336 471 606
	οικουντων	οικουν 336
8:21	απηγαγεν	απηγαγε 149 260 336 471 606 629
	α	ας 149 260 336 471 606 629 769
	εγεννησαν	εγεννησεν 471
8:22	εποιησαν	επλησαν 471

Collation   23

	κατα	ατα 471.
	ακαθαρσιας	ακαρθαρσαις 769
	εμιαναν	εμιανεν 253 655 659
8:23	εθνεσιν	εθνεσι 149 260 336 471 606 629 769
	αυτων	αυτον 659
8:24	αινετος	αυτος 655* 659
	γην	- 336
8:25	δη	δε 655 659
	ειδοσαν	ειδον 149 260 336 471 606 629 769
	ημων	αυτων 149 260 471 606
8:26	της δικαιοσυνης	την δικαιοσυνην 253 655 659
	παιδεια	παιδια 655 659
		παιδαις 769
8:27	επιστρεφον	πιστρεφον 471
	οικτιρησον	οικτιρεισον 149 253 260 606 629 769
		οικτειρησον 471 655 659
8:28	Ισραηλ	Ιερουσαλημ 629*
	ελεους	ελεου 149 260 336 471 606 769
		ελαιου 606
	η	- 253 655 659
	πιστις	πιστης 659
	μεθ'	μετα 149 253 260 336 471 606 655 659
		μετ' 659
8:29	ημεις	ημει 659
	εσκληρυναμεν	εσκληρυνημεν 655 659
	τον	- 253 655 659
8:30	υπεριδης	υπεριδες 659
	καταπιωσιν	καταπιη 149 260 336 471 606 629 769
	ως	- 149 260 336 471 606 629 769
8:31	η ελπις ημων	ηλπισαμεν 149 260 336 471 606 629 769
8:32	ημεις	ημας 655 659
	εφ'	εις 253 655 659
8:33	η	- 629 769
	ευδοκια	+ αυτων 336
	κυριε	κυριος 336 629 769
	σαλευθησομεθα	σαλευθη 659
8:34	στοματι	στομασιν 336
	και	+ συ 149 260 471 606
9:1	εν	ν 471
	απαχθηναι	απελθηναι 655 659
	Ισραηλ	Ιερουσαλημ 336
	αποικεσια	αποικησια 149 260 471 606
	αποστηναι	αποστηνα 471
	κυριου	θεου 655 659
	απερριφησαν	απεριφησαν 253
		απεριψεισαν 655 659
	αυτοις	αυτων 655 659
9:2	εθνει	εθνη 253 655 659
	η	επι 149 260 471 606
	ινα	ιν 253 659
	δικαιωθης	δικαιοσης 253 655 659
	τη	- 336
	κριτης	κριτις 655 659
9:3	κρυβησεται (1)	κριβυβησεται 655
		κριβυθησεται 659
	γνωσεως	γνωσσεως 769
	αδικα	κακα 149 260 336 471 606 629 769
	αι	- 769
	κρυβησεται (2)	κρυβησεται 659
9:4	ημων (1)	μων 471
	εν	- 253 655 659

24   Psalms of Solomon

	δικαιοσυνη	δικαιοσυνης 769
	επισκεπτη	επισκεπη 655 659
9:5	ζωην	τω εν 655 659
	αυτω	εαυτω 149 260 336 471 606 629 769
	αδικιαν	αδικα 149 260 471 606
	κατ'	και 659
9:6	χρηστευση	χρησιμευσει 336
		χρηστευσει 629 769
	ο	- 471
	μη	μει 655
	καθαριεις	καθαρισει all witnesses
	εξαγοριαις	εξηγοριαις 149 260 471 606 629 769
		αξαγοριαις 336
		εξαγοριαν 655 659
	απαντων	παντων 336
9:7	αφησεις	αφησει 149 260 336 471 606 629 769
		αφεσει 253
		αφησι 655 659
	ει	εη 655
	ημαρτηκοσιν	ημαρτηκοσι 149 253 260 336 471 606 629 655 659
	ευθυνεις	ευθυνει 655 659
	ημαρτοσαν	ημαρτον 149 260 336 471 606 629 769
	επι	περι all witnesses
	μεταμελεια	μεταμελια 655 659
9:8	και	αι 471
	συ	σοι 336
	λαος	+ σου 253 655 659
	ημεις	ημης 655
	οικτιρησον	οικτειρον 149 260 336 471 606 629 769
		οικτειρησον 253 655 659
	θεος (2)	+ το 655c
	αποστησης	+ το 659
	ελεος	ελεον 149 260 336 471 606 629 769
9:9	ουκ	ου all witnesses
	απωση	καταπαυση 149 260 471 606 629 769
		καταπαυσεις 253
		καταπαυσει 336
		καταπαυσης 655 659
	εις	- 253 655 659*
		εις τον 659c
9:10	ημεις	ημας 655 659
9:11	η	- 253 629 655 659
	ελεημοσυνη	ελεμοσυνη 253
		ελεημωσυνη 655
	οικον	οικου 655 659
	ετι	εις τον αιωνα του αιωνος 655
10:1	μακαριος	ακαριος 471
	εκυκλωθη	εκακλωθη 769
	μαστιγι	μαστιγη 655 659
		+ και 149 260 471 606 629 769
	πληθυναι	πλθυναι 336
10:2	μαστιγας	+ και 253 655 659
	χρηστος	χριστος 655 659
	γαρ	και 655 659
		- 629 769
	υπομενουσιν	υπομενουσι 149 260 336 471 606 629 659 769
10:3	διαστρεφει	διαπρεφει 253 655
		διατρεφει 659
	αγαπωντας	αγαποντας 253

Collation   25

10:4	μνηστησεται	μνησεται 253 655 659
	των δουλων	του δουλου 655 659
	γαρ	- 149 260 471 606
	νομω	ο μω 655 659
10:5	δικαιος	ικαιος 471
	ο	- 253 655 659
	εν (1)	- 149 253 260 471 606 629 655 659 769
	αινεσει	ενεσει 769*
		αιενεσει 769c
	τω ονοματι	το ονομα 149 260 471 606
	κυριου	+ εις τον αιωνα 336
10:6	οσιοι	οτιοι 253*
		οσιος 659
	εκκλησια	εκλησια 655
10:7	δοξασουσιν	δοξασουσι 149 260 471 606 629 769
		δοξασωσι 336
10:8	η σωτηρια	- 655 659
	οικον	οικου 655 659
	εις ευφροσυνην	εις σωφροσυνην 149 260 471 606 655 659
		εισωφροσθνην 253
11:1	σαλπισατε	αλπισατε 471
	ηλεησεν	ελεησεν 659 769
	θεος	+ εν 149 260 471 606
	αυτων	αυτου 336
11:2	τα	- 336
	εις	- 336
	υπο	απο 253 655 659
11:4	ορη	οροι 336
	εφυγοσαν	εφυγον 149 260 336 471 606 629 769
11:5	οι δρυμοι εσκιασαν αυτοις εν τη παροδω αυτων	
		- 655 659
	δρυμοι	βουνοι 629
		δριμοι 769
	εσκιασαν	εσκιρτησαν 471 606
	ξυλον	ξυλων 659
11:6	παρελθη	+ ο 659
11:7	ενδυσαι	νδυσαι 471
		ενδυσας 655 659
	ιματια	ιματι 659
	ετοιμασον	τοιμασον 336
	Ισραηλ	- 629 769
	ετι	+ οιη 629*
		+ Ισραηλ 629c 769
11:8	και	+ εν 149 260 471 606
12:1	κυριε	ε 471 (initial letter of abbreviation κε omitted)
	ψιθυρου	ψυθυρου 655*
	δολια	πονερα 629*
		δολερα 769
12:2	ποικιλια	ποιησει 149 260 471 606
		τη κυλια 655 659*
		ποικλησι 659c
	στροφης	διαστροφης 149 260 471 606
		τροφης 629 769
	γλωσσης	γλωσης 769
	λαω	αλω 149 260 471
		αλλω 606
	αναπτον	αναπτων 336
	καλλονην	καλαμην 149 260 471 606
		καλονην 655 659

26   Psalms of Solomon

12:3	εμπρησαι	εμπλησαι all witnesses
	ψευδει	ψευδη 336
	παρανομους	παρανομου 149 260 336 471 606
	συγχεαι οικους	συγχεαι παρανομους οικους 149 260 471 606
		συνχεαι οικους παρανομους 253 655 659
		συγχεαι οικους παρανπμους 336 629 769
	χειλεσιν	χειλεσι 149 260 336 471 606 629
		ιχηλεσι 769
	ψιθυροις	ψιθυρων 336
12:4	μακρυναι	ακρυναι 471
	ακακων	κακων 606
	σκορπισθειησαν	σκορπισθειη 149 260 336 471 606 629 769
	απολοιτο	απωλοιτο 336
12:5	φυλαξαι	pr συγχεαι οικους και 253 655 659
	ψυχην ησουχιον μισουσαν αδικους και κατευθυναι κυριος	
		- 253 655 659
	ανδρα	ανδρος 253 655 659
	ποιουντα	ποιουντος 253 655 659
12:6	επι	εστι 769
	παιδα	παιδων 336
	οι	η 655 659
	αμαρτωλοι	αμαρτλοι 471
	και (2)	+ οι 336 769
	οσιοι	οσοι 655 659
	κληρονομησαισαν	κληρονομησαιεν 149 260 336 471 606 629 769
		κληρονομισαισαν 253
		κληρονομησασαν 655 659
	επαγγελιας	επαγγελειας 655 659
	κυριου (4)	- 253 655 659
13:1	δεξια	εξια 471
	εσκεπασεν	εσκεπασε 149 260 336 471 606 629 769
13:2	ρομφαιας διαπορευμενης	
		obliterated 769[16]
	ρομφαιας	ρομφαια 655 659
	και θανατου αμαρτωλων	
		obliterated 769
13:3	επεδραμοσαν	επεδραμον 149 260 336 471 606
		επεδραμουσαν 655 659
		629 illegible
	ετιλλοσαν	ετιλλον 149 260 336 471 606
		ετειλον 629
		επιλλοσαν 659
	μυλαις	+ αυτων 149 260 471 606
	εθλων	+ τα 336
13:4	ημας	+ ο 336 629
13:5	εταραχθη	ταραχθη 471
	ευσεβης	ασεβης 471
	τα	- 253 655 659
13:6	δεινη	δινη 253 655 659
	η	- 336 471 606 629 769
	αψεται	+ του 629 769
	ουδεν	- 149 260 336 471 606 629 769
	εκ παντων τουτων	- 629
	τουτων	+ ουδεν 149 260 336 471 606
13:7	entire verse	- 629 769
	παιδεια	παιδια 655 659
	των αμαρτωλων	του αμαρτωλου 253 655 659
13:8	ινα	να 336
13:9	παιδεια	παιδια 655 659

Collation   27

                πρωτοτοκου   πρπτοτοκου 253 659
13:10   οτι   τι 336
        φεισεται   φησεται 659
        παιδεια   παιδια 655 659
13:11   αμαρτωλοι   μαρτωλοι 336
        και   αι 336
        ουχ   ουκ 253 659
13:12   αυτον   - 253 655 659
14:1   πιστος   ιστος 471
        υπομενουσιν   υπομενουσι 149 260 336 471 606 629 769
        παιδειαν   παιδιαν 655 659
14:2   πορευμενος   + εν ακακια και 336
        ω   ως 149 260 471 606
                                ον 336
                                - 253 655 659
        ημιν   ημειν 655
14:2   οσιοι (1)   σιοι 471
                                οσιοει 655
        κυριου (1)   θεου 655c 659c
        του   - 149 260 336 471 606 629 769
        αυτου   αυτα 655 659
14:4   φυτεια   φυτια 655 659
        ερριζωμενη   ερριζομενη 253 655 659
        εκτιλησονται   εκτειλησονται 253 655 659
                                εκτιλλησονται 336
14:5   μερις   μερι 659
        και   + η 149 260 336 471 606 655 659
        εστιν   + ο 149 260 471 606
14:6   και   αι 471
14:7   η   εν 149 260 471 606
        του θεου   αυτου 629
                                - θεου 769
14:8   οδοι   οδος 655 659
        και   + τα 629 769
        ταμιεια   ταμεια 253 655 659
14:9   σκοτος   σκοτως 659
        ουχ   ουκ 655 659
        ελεους   ελεου 149 260 471 606 629 769
14:10   κληρονομησουσιν   κλυρονομησουσι 149 260 471 606 629
15:1   εν   ν 471
        τω   του 655 659
        εις   + την 336
        ηλπισα   εσωθην 253 655 659c
                                - 659*
        συ   + ει 336
15:2   τις   τι 336
        ισχυει   ισχυσει 336
        σοι   - 336
        τι   το 655 659
        δυνατος   + ο 655 659
        εξομολογησασθαι   εξομολογησασσθαι 336
        τω   τη αληθεια 655
15:3   καινον   και αινον 149 260 471 606
                                629 illegible
        μετα   μετ' 471
        γλωσσης   γνωσσης 655 659
        απαρχην   απαρχης 336
                                απαρχιν 655 659
                                απαρχη 629 769

28   Psalms of Solomon

15:4   πυρος   υρος 471
        οργη   - 629 769
        ουχ   ουκ 253 655 659
15:5   επι   εφ' 253 655 659
        ολεθρευσαι   ολοθρευσαι 149 260 336 471 606 629 769
                            ολωθρευσαι 655c 659
15:7   λιμος   λυμος 659
        απο δικαιων μακραν
                            μακραν απο δικαιων 149 260 336 471 606 629 769
        διωκομενοι   διωκομενου 149 253 260 471 606 629 655 659 769
                            + απο 253 655 659
        πολεμου   λιμου 149 253 260 471 606 629 769
                            λυμου 655 659
        οσιων   θειων 336 629 769
15:8   καταδιωξονται   καταδιωξεται 149 260 336 471 606 629 769
                            + γαρ ως 655 659
        δε   ε 471
                            + ωκομενου 655[17]
        καταλημψονται   καταληψεται 149 260 336 471 606 629 769
                            κατταληψονται 655
                            καταληψονται 659
        ποιουντες   πιουντες 769
        κυριου   του θεου 629 769
15:9   λαταλημφθησονται   καταληφθησονται 149 253c 260 471 606 655 659
                            καταληφθησηται 629
        απωλειας   απολειας 336
        μετωπου   μετοπου 336
15:10   απωλεια   απολεια 253 655 659
        αι   - 253 655 659
        κατω   κατωτατου 336
15:11   ουχ   ουκ 655 659
        αυτων (2)   αυτου 655 659
        αι   και 336
        αμαρτιαι   ανομιαι 149 260 336 471 606 629 769
        εξερημωσουσιν   εξερημωσωσιν 253
                            εξερημωσιν 655 659
15:12   απολουνται   + οι 149 260 471 606
        οταν   οι αν 655 659
        επισκεπτηται   επεσκεπτηται 655 659
        αυτου   + αποδουνται αμαρτωλοις εις τον αιωνα χρονον
                              149 260 471 606
15:13   ζησονται   ζησωνται 655 659
        και αμαρτωλοι απολουνται εις τον αιωνα χρονου
                            - 149 260 471 606
        αμαρτωλοι απολουνται
                            απολουνται αμαρτωλοι 336
                            απολουνται οι αμαρτωλοι 629 769
16:1   τω   το 336
                            629 illegible
        νυσταξαι   νησταξαι 655 659
        ψυχην   ψυχη 655 659
        ωλισθησα   υπνωσα 336
                            ωλισεησα 655
        εν (2)   ω 471
                            - 629 769
        καταφορα   καταφθορα 149 260 336 471 629 769
        υπνουντων   υπνου τω all witnesses
        μακραν   + γενεσθαι 336
16:2   συνεγγυς   συηγγος 655 659
16:3   διενεχθηναι   διανεχθηναι 655 659

Collation   29

           ψυχην   ψυχη 655 659
           κυριος   θεος 336
           μου (2)   + εις σωτηριαν 336
16:4   entire verse   - 336
           ενυξεν   ενυξε 149 260 471 606 629
           ο   ως 659
           εσωσεν   εσωσε 149 260 471 606 629
16:5   εξομολογησομαι σοι ο θεος οτι αντελαβου μου εις σωτηριαν
                                - 336
           εξομολογησομαι   εξομολοησομαι 471
           σοι   σι 655 659
           αντελαβου   αντελαβετο 253 655 659
           ελογισω με   ελογησωμαι 253
                                ελογησομαι 336
                                ελογησωμεν 655 659
                                ελογισομαι 769*
                                ελογισο με 769c
16:6   αποστησης   αποστησεις 655 659
           μνημην   + περι 253 655 659
           σου (2)   του 655 659
           μου   - 253 655 659
16:7   απο αμαρτιας πονηρας και απο πασης γυναικος πονηρας σκανδαλιζουσης
           αφρονα   - 336
16:8   και (1)   - 336
           υποκειμενου   αποκειμενου 655 659
           απο αμαρτιας   continuation of text illegible 629
           ανωφελους   ανοφελους 253 336 655 659
16:9   χειρων   ειρων 471
           τοπω   τωπω 336
16:10   λογους   λογης 655*
           περιστειλον   περιστειλους 471
16:11   γογγυσμον και ολιγοψυχιαν εν θλιψει μακρυνον απ' εμου
                                - 769
           ολιγοψυχιαν   ολιγωψυχιαν 336
           σε   ε 471
16:12   στηρισον   στηριξον 149 260 471 606
                                στηρξον 769
           εν τω ενισχυσαι σε την ψυχην μου
                                - 659
           εωισχυσαι   ισχυσαι 606
16:13   παιδειαν εν πενια
                                εν πενια παιδειαν 149* 260* 471 606[18]
           παιδειαν   πεδιαν 253 659
                                πεδιεαν 655
16:14   ελεγχεσθαι   ελεχεσθαι 655 659
           αυτου   αυτης 149 260 471 606 769
           σαρκι   σαρκη 655 659
17:1   κυριε   ε 471 (initial letter of abbreviation κε omitted)
           αυτος   - 253 655 659
           ημων (1)   + εις τον αιωνα ο θεος ημων και 336
           θεος   + ημων 253 655 659
17:2   και   3004 begins
17:3   ημεις   ημας 655 659
           ελπιουμεν   ελπιζομεν 336
           τον θεον   θεον τον 149 260 336 471 606
                                τον θεον τον 769 3004
           ελεους   ελεου 149 260 336 471 606 769 3004
           εν κρισει   - 253 655 659

30   Psalms of Solomon

17:4   ηρετισω   ηρετησω 253 655 659
                                ρετισω 471
        αυτου (1)   - 253 655 659
        εκλειπειν   εκλιπειν 336 471
        σου   το 769
        βασιλειον   βασιλιον 659
17:5   ημιν (1)   ημων 336
        επεθεντο   υπεθεντο 336
        εξωσαν   εξωσαντο 253 655 659
                                εξωσοη 471
        ουκ   - 769
        επηγγειλω   επιγγειλω 253 336
                                + και 336
        μετα   μετα μετα 655
        αφειλαντο   αφειλοντο 149 260 336 471 606 769 3004
17:6   δοξη   δοξει 659
        ηρημωσαν   ερημωσαν 336 3004*
        υπερηφανια   υπερυφανια 659
        αλλαγματος   αλαλαγματος 149 260 471 606 3004
17:7   το   - 253 655 659
17:8   αποδωσεις   αφοδωσεις 471
        ευρεθηναι   ευρεθειη 149 260 471 606 3004
17:9   κατα το εργα αυτων
                                - 253
        ουκ (1)   - 149 260 471 606 3004
        ηλεησεν   ελεησει all witnesses
        εξηρευνησεν   εξηρευννησε 149 260 336 471 606 3004
        αυτων ενα   αυτοις 149 260 471 606 3004
17:10   κυριος   θεος 336
        ποιει   εποιησεν 336
        επι   - 655 659
17:11   ηρημωσεν ο ανομος την γην
                                - 659
        ηρημωσεν   ερημωσεν 336
        ανομος   ανεμος 149 260 471 606 3004
                                + επι 655
        πρεσβυτην   πρησβυτην 655
        και (2)   + τα 336 3004
17:12   αυτου   αυτων 336
        εμπαιγμον   εμπεγμον 253 655 659
        και (2)   - 3004*
        εφεισατο   εφησατο 655 659
17:13   ετοιησεν   ετοιησε 336
        υπερηφανιαν   εν υπερηφανια 253 336 659
                                υπερηφανια 655
        αλλοτρια   αποτρια 471
        του   - 336
17:14   εποιησεν   + ο θεος 655 659
        του σθενους   τοις θεοις all witnesses
17:15   επεκρατουσαν   επεκρατουν 149 260 471 606 3004
                                απεκρατουν 336
        υιοι   - 655
        εν αυτοις ο ποιων εν
                                εν αυτοις εν μεσω 149 260 336 471 606 769 3004
                                εν μεσω εν αυτοις 253 655 659
        εφυγοσαν   εφυγον 149 260 336 471 606 769 3004
        απ' αυτων   απο τουτου 769
        οσιων   - 769
        στρουθια   στρουθιοι 655 659
        εξεπεταστησαν   εξεπετασαν 769

Collation

17:17	ψυχη	ψυχης 655 659
	σεσωσμενη	εωσμενη 655 659
	αυτων	+ εφυγον (εφυγοσαν 655 659) απ' αυτων οι αγαπωντης συναγωγας οσιων 253 655 659
17:18	ο (1)	- 253 655 659
	υπο	υπ' 655 659
	ανεσχεν	ενεσχεν 336
	του	τους 655 659
	την γην	της γης 336
17:19	πηγαι	pr αι 3004
	συνεσχεθησαν	συνεχεθησαν 655 659
17:20	αυτων	αυτου 336
	αμαρτια	+ εις τον καιρον ον οιδας συ ο θεος του βασιλευσαι επι Ισραηλ παιδα σου 336
	κριτης	κριθεις 655 659
17:21	αυτων	αυτον 769
	υιον	υιω 655 659
	Δαυιδ	Δαβιδ 655 659
	εις τον καιρον, ον ειλου συ, ο θεος, του βασιλευσαι επι Ισραηλ παιδα σου	- 336
	ειλου	οιδες 149 260
		ιδες 253 659
		οιδας 471 606 3004
		ιδευ 655
		ειδες 769
	βασιλευσαι	βασιλευσας 655
	επι	- 769
17:22	ισχυν	ισχην 655
	καθαρισαι	καθαρισον all witnesses
	εθνων	εθνον 659*
	καταπατουντων	και απατουντων 3004*
	απωλεια	+ και 655 659
17:23	δικαιοσυνης	εν δικαιοσυνη all witnesses
	εξωσαι	εξωσον 336 769
		εξωσαν 655 659
	εκτριψαι	εκτριψας 655 659
	υπερηφανιαν	υπερηφανιαν 655
	αμαρτωλου	αμαρτωλους 149 260 606 3004*
		αμαρτωλων 336
	ως σκευη	εν σκευη 336
		ω σκευη 655 769 (ωσκευη 655)
17:24	συντριψαι	συντριψον 336
17:25	εν απειλη αυτου φυγειν εθνη απο προσωπου αυτου	- 471 3004*
	απειλη	απελλη 3004c
17:26	ηγιασμενου	- 655 659
17:27	αυλισθηναι	+ ετι 253 655 659
	αυτων (2)	αυτον 655*
	παντες	παντας 655 659
	εισιν αυτων	αυτων εισι 149 260 471 606
		αυτων εισιν 336 769 3004
17:28	αυτων	αυτον 655c
	αλλογενης	αλλογενες 655 659
	παροικησει	+ εν 769
17:29	διαψαλμα	- 471 3004*
17:30	και (1)	+ εξ 655 659
	υπο	κυπο 655
	τον	- 149 260 336 471 606 655 659 769 3004
	καθαριει	καθαρισει 149 260 336 471 606 3004
		κιθαριει 655 659

32   Psalms of Solomon

         το   τω 3004*
17:31   ερχεσθαι   ερχεσθε 336 769
         απ'   απο 659
         φεροντες   φερωντες 659
         εξησθενηκοτας   εξοσθενηκοτας 659
         ιδειν   ιδεν 769
         ην   ειν 655 659
         αυτην   αυτη 659*
17:32   δικαιος   + και 606
         επ'   υπ' 3004*
         εστιν   + η 655 659
         αυτων   αυτον 655* 659*
         οτι παντες αγιοι,   και βασιλευς αυτων χριστος κυριου
                                 - 336
         χριστος κυριου   χριστος κυριος
                                 149 253 260 471 606 655 659 769 3004
17:33   επι   εφ'
         ουδε (1)   ουδεν 655
         πληθυνει   πληθυνω 655 659
         ουδε (2)   και 149 260 336 471 606 769 3004
         λαους   - all witnesses
         ελπιδας   ελπιδα 3004*
         εις   ες 659
17:34   ελπις   ελπιξ 655*
         του   + αυτου 253 655 659
17:35   παταξει   καταξει 253 336 655 659
         εις   + τον 336
17:36   απο   επ' 655 659
         λαου μεγαλου   λαους μεγαλους 253 655 659
         ισχυι   ισχυει 253 659
17:37   ασθενησει   ανθενησει 659*
         κατειργασατο   κατηργασατο 655 659
         δυνατον   δυναμιν 769
                                 - 336
         μετα   μετ' all witnesses
         δικαιοσυνης   δικαιοσυνην 253 655* 659
17:38   και (1)   - 659
         ισχυι   ισχυει 253 655 659
17:39   η   - 606
17:40   και (1)   - 655 659
         φοβω   φοβον 655 659
         ποιμαινων   ποιμενων 655 659
         δικαιοσυνη   δικαιοσυνην 655 659
         αφησει   αφησαι 336
         εν τη νομη αυτων   - 655 659
         αυτων   αυτω 769
17:41   εω ισοτητι παντας   αυτους
                                 - 655 659
         ισοτητι   οσιοτητι 149 260 471 606 769* 3004
         αξει   αυξει 606
                                 ηξει 655* 659*
         υπερηφανια   υπερυφανια 655 659
                                 υπερηφανεια 3004*
         καταδυναστευθηναι
                                 καταδυναστευθυναι 655
         αυτοις   αυτω 3004* (corrected by same hand)
17:42   Ισραηλ   Ιερουσαλημ 336
17:43   το πρωτον τιμιον   τιμιον το πρωτον 149 260 336 471 606 769 3004
         συναγωγαις   συναγωγας 655*
         διακρινει   διακρινεις 3004*

Collation

	λαου	λαους 149 260 336 471 606 769 3004
	ηγιασμενου	ηγιασμενων 149 260 471 606 3004
	αυτου	αυτον 253
		αυτων 655 659
	ως	- 336
17:44	γενομενοι	γινομενοι 149 260 336 471 606c 769 3004
		γινομαι 606*
	Ισραηλ	Ιερουσαλημ 336
	α ποιησει	ποιησαι 253 336 655 659 769
17:45	ταχυναι	ταχυνη 253 655 659
	ρυσαιτο	ρυσεται 149 253 260 336 471 606 655 659 3004
		ρυσαι 769
	ακαθαρσιας	ακαρθασιας 769
17:46	βασιλευς	βασιλεος 655 659
18:1	μετα	επι 253 655 659
	δοματος	δηματος 659
18:2	επιβλεποντες	επιβλεπουσιν 769
	ουχ	ουκ 655 659
	εξ	ες 655 659
	αυτων	αυτον 655* 659*
18:3	ελεους	ελεου 149 260 336 471 606 769 3004
	σπερμα	σπερματα 655 659
	υιους	υιου all witnesses
18:4	η	- 253
	παιδεια	παιδια 253 659
	πρωτοτοκον	πρωτοτοκου 769
	μονογενη	μονογενους 769
	ευηκοον	υπηκοον 149 260 471 606 3004
	αμαθιας	αμαθειας 336
	αγνοια	336 omits remaining text; MS continues with Sirach 33[19]
18:5	καθαρισαι	καθαριση 253 655 659
	ελεους	ελεου 149 260 471 606 769 3004
		ελεος 655 659
	αναξει	αινεσει 3004*
18:6	γενομενοι	γινομενοι 149 260 471 606 769 3004
	ταις	- 253 659
18:7	υπο	απο 3004*
	παιδειας	απαιδιας 655 659
18:8	ανδρα	ανδρας 253 655 659
	ενωπιον	εν φοβω 149 260 471 606 3004
18:9	ελεους	ελεου 149 260 471 606 769 3004
	διαψαλμα	διαψαλμ 149 253 260 655 659
		- 471 3004*[20]
18:10	ημων ο θεος	ο θεος ημων 149 260 471 606 769 3004
	πορεια	πορια 253 655 659
	φωστηρας	ημερας 3004
18:11	οδος	οδως 655*
	αυτων	αυτοι 655*
18:12	οδων	απο οδου 149 260 471 606 769 3004
	αυτων	- 3004*

CHAPTER THREE

MANUSCRIPT GROUPINGS

A necessary step in reconstructing the history of the transmission of a writing is to arrange its extant witnesses into textual groups of families.[1] The determination of these relationships is accomplished by a careful examination of the readings of the MSS, and is governed by the principle that, "apart from accident, identity of reading implies identity of origin."[2]

VON GEBHARDT'S STEMMA

Von Gebhardt summarized the relationship which he found among the MSS of the *PssSol* by means of the following stemma.[3]

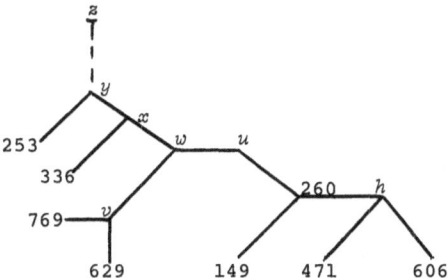

In this diagram, z denotes the Greek archetype of the *PssSol*. The ancestral texts of 253 and 336 are y and x, respectively.[4] The ancestral text behind 629 and 769 is w, and v is their immediate common forebear.[5] The ancestral text of the group 149-260-471-606 is u.[6] As one may observe from this schema, Von Gebhardt believes that 260 is the MS from which all other members of the group have been directly or indirectly copied.[7] The intermediate MS between 260 and 471-606 is represented by h.[8] Von Gebhardt identified w, x, and y as uncial MSS;[9] h, u, and v are miniscules.[10]

35

Von Gebhardt identified two text groups: 149-260-471-606 and 629-769.[11] MSS 253 and 336 are singular witnesses, each of which preserves a large number of readings found in no other MSS.[12] Although 253 and 336 do not form a text group, they share many readings in common,[13] and are related in that the ancestor of 336 is descended from that of 253.

The remainder of this chapter will employ the Claremont Profile Method to examine further the groupings of the witnesses. This examination will provide an independent confirmation of von Gebhardt's groupings and will identify in terms of their group membership those MSS which were not examined by von Gebhardt: 655, 659, and 3004.

THE CLAREMONT PROFILE METHOD

The CPM was first described by E. J. Epp in a paper read before the Pacific Coast Section of the Society of Biblical Literature in May, 1967, in which the CPM was declared to be a "major breakthrough" in grouping New Testament miniscule MSS.[14] The CPM was endorsed and illustrated by E. C. Colwell in his 1968 status report on the International Greek New Testament Project.[15] Complete descriptions of the method, its development, and its applications are found in its developers' dissertations: P. R. McReynolds' "The Claremont Profile Method and the Grouping of Byzantine New Testament Manuscripts,"[16] and F. Wisse's "The Claremont Profile Method for the Classification of Byzantine New Testament Manuscripts: a Study in Method.[17]

The CPM was developed in response to the need of the International Greek New Testament Project for a rapid and accurate means of observing the group relationship among a large number of previously unclassified Greek MSS.[18] In addition, those working on the project found it necessary to avoid dependence on the previous MS groupings of von Soden, whose work they had found to be untrustworthy.[19] Wisse has summarized the need for a new method:

> ...a method would have to be developed which would test all known groups, and spot the members which could best represent the whole group. This method would have to be independent from von Soden in order to quiet the suspicions

Manuscript Groupings   37

of friends and critics. The method should ideally be a
rapid sampling tool so that many uncollated MSS could be
checked for group membership and total value.[20]

The CPM was developed from the realization that, although
some groups of MSS never contain readings which are not shared
with other text types, they are nevertheless identifiable in
terms of the total patterns of agreement and disagreement which
appear with regard to other text types.[21] These agreements and
disagreements are profiled by the CPM in a graphic form by means
of which the evidence of groups and the identity of their constituent MSS may be observed.[22]

The following outline describes the steps necessary for
implementing the CPM:

(1) The MSS to be examined are collated against a stan-
dard base text. The collations of the Internaitional Greek New
Testament Project were made against the *textus receptus*. This
text has been traditionally used as a collation base, and has
the advantage of resembling the text of Byzantine MSS and thus
of simplifying the task of collation. Wisse notes, however,
that the collation base is merely a tool for comparing the readings of the witnesses, and that any text may be used.[23] The
collations to be used in the CPM are checked at least twice for
accuracy.[24]

(2) Variant readings which are probably the result of
scribal error, misspelling, or other orthographic peculiarity
are excluded. These include itacisms, the use of the final *nu*
or *sigma*, breathing marks, abbreviations, common vowel changes,
and word division.[25] Common scribal variants may not be used as
evidence of a genetic connection among witnesses, and may in
fact obscure the genuine relationship among them.[26]

(3) Singular readings are excluded. Readings found in
only one MS have a high probability of being scribal errors, and
thus cannot shed light on the relationship among the witnesses.[27]

(4) Readings supported by two-thirds of the members of
all known text groups are excluded. These readings cannot aid
in differentiating among groups.[28]

(5) Care is taken to include all distinct variations of
those which remain and also the entire unit of each variation.
In the former case, all multiple variant readings at the same
point in the text are to be noted.[29] In the latter case, changes

in a pronoun as a result of a verb change are considered part of the same unit of variation.[30]

(6) The readings thus selected are assembled into a graph by means of which the MSS supporting each may be observed. These readings are called "test readings." A text group is defined by the presence of readings where two-thirds of the MSS of that group agree, and by the observation of a distinct profile of readings.[31] The failure of two alleged groups to demonstrate profiles different from one another is an indication that they are in reality the same group.[32]

On the following pages the CPM will be applied to the Greek text of the *PssSol*. It will be noted that the purposes of this application will be among those for which the CPM was devised: to provide a confirmation of MS groupings independently of previous research,[33] and to identify new textual witnesses in terms of their group affinities.[34]

THE CLAREMONT PROFILE METHOD AND THE PSALMS OF SOLOMON

The witnesses to the Greek text of the *PssSol* have been collated in the previous chapter. Since no *textus receptus* for the *PssSol* exists,[35] this collation was made against the text of the Psalms in Rahlfs' *Septuaginta*.[36] This text is the most readily available Greek text of the *PssSol*.

Variant readings which were probably the result of scribal error or other orthographic variations were excluded. In addition to those categories named by McReynolds,[37] all instances of "errors arising from faulty eyesight" and "errors arising from faulty hearing" listed in Bruce M. Metzger's *The Text of the New Testament* were also omitted.[38] Examples of excluded readings include those resulting from confusion of the letters *epsilon, theta, omicron,* and *sigma*: 3:11 επισκοπηται, 4:12 ολοθρευσαι, 5:2 ευχρηστος, 9:2 δικαιος, and 17:11 ανεμος. Ειτα at 8:6 was excluded as the probable result of confusion between a *pi* and a *tau*. Several readings arose from the confusion of an *omicron* and an *omega*: 2:32 κρινον, 3:5 εδικαιοσαν, 4:5 εισωδω, 8:8 εναντιων, 10:3 αγαποντας, and 15:5 ολωθρευσαι are examples. The diphthong *alpha iota* was confused with the *epsilon*, resulting in readings including: 2:11 εμπεγμον, 2:24 εκχαιε, 5:1

Manuscript Groupings   39

εναισω, 8:12 αφαιδρω/αφαιδρων and 17:12 εμπεγμον. Itacisms
occurred frequently in the witnesses: 2:8 πρεσβητην, 2:17
εξηλιψας, 2:19 ωνιδησαν, 2:21 απερριφει, 2:23 μνησεως, 2:23
επιτιμησεις, and 2:25 χρονησης are only a few examples. An
interesting series of variations occurs at 16:5, where all the
variants against ελογισω με involve combinations of *omicron/
omega*, *alpha iota/epsilon*, and *eta/iota* changes. All of these
variant readings were therefore omitted. Variant readings of
other varieties than those listed by McReynolds and by Metzger
were retained.[39]

All singular readings were excluded. A large number of
these readings were instances where MS 471 omits the initial
letter of a word: 1:1 βοησα, 2:1 ν, 2:11 στησε, 8:1 λιψιν, 8:6
ατευθυνουσιν, 8:22 ατα, and 9:8 αι are examples.

It was not possible to observe the CPM's principle of
excluding readings supported by two-thirds of the members of
each known group, since von Gebhardt's work had identified only
two groups, of which the smaller had only two members. All
readings supported by all the MSS against a conjectural reading
were excluded.[40] In addition, all other readings were omitted
which were supported by the remaining MSS once a singular reading was excluded. This was the case in 9:7 once the singular
reading αφεσει and the itacism αφησι were omitted, and at 17:45
when the singular reading ρυσαι was excluded.

With the exception of the foregoing exclusions, all other
distinct variant readings were included. The principle of excluding scribal errors and other orthographic variants requires
combining multiple readings when the differences between them
are exclusively made up of such factors. When, for example,
the reading καθησε βεβηλε at 4:1 is recognized to be due to a
common scribal variation on καθησαι βεβηλε,[41] both variants must
be taken to form one distinct variation against the reading
βεβηλε, καθησαι. This is also true of 4:21 παρωξυνεν/παρωξηνεν,
6:4 ευλογησε/ευλογησεν, 8:8 ανακαλυψεν/ανακαληψεν, 10:3 δια-
τρεψρι/διαπρεψει, and 15:8 κατταληφονται/καταληφονται. The omission of itacism from consideration reduces the four readings at
9:9 to two: καταπαυση/καταπαυσει and καταπαυσεις/καταπαυσης.
The significant variant is the presence of absence of the final
sigma.

An important departure from the procedure of McReynolds and Wisse was taken in applying the CPM to the *PsSol*. Because of the quantity of MS evidence for the Gospel of Luke, the writing to which the CPM was first applied, it was impossible for its developers to profile the entire gospel. Sample chapters from the beginning, middle, and end were selected to represent the text of the entire writing.[42] By selecting these chapters, McReynolds and Wisse were confident of detecting block mixture or changes in the exemplar of their witnesses,[43] without having to profile the readings of the entire gospel.[44] Compared to the large number of witnesses to the text of Luke, there exist only a few MSS of the *PsSol*. It was therefore practical to avoid dependence on sample chapters and to profile the text of all eighteen Psalms. By following this procedure, any instances of block mixture which might have occurred between sampled sections would have been detected.[45]

THE PROFILE OF THE PSALMS OF SOLOMON

The following is the profile of the text readings of the *PsSol* according to the CPM. Variant readings are identified by chapter and verse and, by lower case letters, by the corresponding entry in the collation.[46] The witnesses, including those not included by von Gebhardt, have been listed according to their tentative groupings.[47] Since an initial inspection of the collation shows a number of readings at which 655 and 659 agree with 253, and at which 3004 agrees with members of the 260 group, the MSS have been arranged accordingly. An x indicates that the MS agrees with the test reading. An o indicates either that the MS has a lacuna at that point, or that the MS departs from both the test reading and the collation base. Agreements with the collation base against the test reading appear as a blank.[48] When a witness has been corrected, an asterisk indicates the original reading and a o the correction.

Manuscript Groupings 41

TEST READINGS		253	655	659	336	MANU629	SCR769	IPT149	S 260	471	606	3004
1:1	b	x	x	x		o						o
1:4	a		x	x		o						o
1:5	a		x	x		o						o
2:2	a		o	o	x	o	x	x	x	x	x	o
2:3					x	o	x	x	x	x	x	o
2:4	d	o	o	o	o	o	o	x	x	x	x	o
	e	x	o	o	x	o	x	o	o	o	o	o
	f	o	x	x	o	o	o	o	o	o	o	o
2:5	a	x	x	x	x	o	x	x	x		x	o
	b					o		x	x	x	x	o
	d					o		x	x	x	x	o
2:6	a	x	x	x		o						o
	b	x	x	x		o						o
2:7	c		x	x		o						o
2:8	b				x	o	x	x	x	x	x	o
	c				x	o	x	x	x	x	x	o
	g		x	x		o						o
2:9	b		x	x		o						o
	c		x	x		o						o
2:10	a		x	x		o						o
2:11	ac					o		x	x	o	x	o
	e		x	x		o						o
	f	x	x	x		o						o
2:12	b		x	x		o						o
	c		x	x		o						o
2:13	a		x	x		o						o
	b				x	o	x	x	x	x	x	o
2:14					x	o	x					o
2:16	a					o	x	x	x	x	x	o
2:18	b		x	x		o						o
2:19	ef	x	o	o	x	o	x	x	x	x	x	o
2:22	e	x	x	x		o						o
	g		x	x		o						o
	h					o		x	x			o
2:23	a	x	x	x		o						o
	e				x	o	x	x	x	x	x	o
2:24	a	x	x	x		o						o
	c		x	x		o						o
	d	x	x	x	o	o						o
2:26	d		x	x		o						o
2:27	a					o						o
	c				x		x	x	x	x	x	o
2:31	a				x			x	x	x	x	o
	d				x	x	x	x	x	x	x	o
	e		x	x								o
2:32	a				x	x	x	x	x	x	x	o
2:33	b					*	x					o
	c		x	x								o
2:35	a		x	x								o
2:36	b		x	x								o
	c					x		x	x	x	x	o
3:2	c					x	x	x	x	x	x	o
3:3	b	x	x	x								o

42   Psalms of Solomon

		253	655	659	336	629	769	149	260	471	606	3004
3:4	b	x	x	x								o
	c				x	x	x	x	x	x	x	o
3:5	a		x	x								o
	e		x	x								o
	g	x	x	x		*						o
3:6	b		x	x								o
	c				x		x	x	x	x	x	o
3:8	c	x	x	x								o
	d				x	x	x	x	x	x	x	o
	e					x	x					
3:9	c		x	x								o
3:10	a					o		x	x	x	x	o
	c	x	x	x		x	x					o
3:11	a	x	x	x								o
3:12	a				x	x	x	x	x	x	x	o
	b					x	x	x	x	x	x	o
	d	x	x	x	o							o
4:1	ab				x	x	x	x	x		x	o
	c							x	x	x	x	o
4:2	a		x	*								o
	c		x	x	o							o
	d		o	o		o	o	x	x	x	x	o
	e		o	o		x	x	o	o	o	o	o
4:3	a		*	*								o
	c				x	x	x	x	x	x	x	o
	d	x	x	x								o
	e	x	x	x								o
4:4	a	x	x	x								o
	b	x	x	x								o
	f	x	x	x								o
	g	x	x	x								o
	h	x	x	x								o
4:6	b		c	x								o
4:8	a		o	o			x	x	x	x	x	o
	d				x			x	x	x	x	o
	f	x	x	x								o
	g	x	x	x								o
4:9	b							x	x	x	x	o
4:10	a	x	x	x								o
	b							x	x	x	x	o
4:11	a					o		x	x	x	x	o
4:13	d							x	x	x	x	o
4:15	b							x	x	x	x	o
	c	x	x	x								o
	d							x	x	x	x	o
	f			o						x	x	o
4:16	d	o	o	o						x	x	o
	e	o	x	x						o	o	o
	fg		x	x						x	x	o
	h	x	x	x								o
4:17	a	x	x	x								o
4:18	a	x	x	x								o
	b		x	x	x	x	x	x	x	x	x	o
4:19			x	x								o

Manuscript Groupings   43

		253	655	659	336	629	769	149	260	471	606	3004
4:20	a				x	x	x	x	x	x	x	o
	b		x	x								o
	c	x	x	x								o
	d					x	x					o
	e	x	x	x								o
	f	x	x	x								o
4:21	b		x	x								o
	c				x			x	x	x	x	o
	ef	x	x	x								o
4:22	a		x	x								o
4:23	a	x	x	x								o
4:24	a		x	x								o
5:1	b				x					x	x	o
5:3	a		x	x								o
	b					x	x					o
	d							x	x	x	x	o
5:4								x	x	x	x	o
5:5	a	x	x	o								o
	cd				x	o		x	x	x	x	o
	f		x	x								o
	g				x	x	x	x	x	x	x	o
5:7	a		x	x								o
5:9	b		o	o	x	x	x	x	x	x	x	o
	c		x	x	o	o	o	o	o	o	o	o
5:10	b		x	x								o
	c		x	x								o
	f					x	x					o
	h					x	x	x	x	x	x	o
5:11	a							x	x	x	x	o
	c	o	x	x								o
5:12	a	x	x	x								o
	b				x			x	x	x	x	o
	ce				x	x	x	x	x	x	x	o
5:13	a	o	o	o		o	o	x	x	x	x	o
	b	x	x	x		x	x	o	o	o	o	o
	c				x			x	x	x	x	o
	e		o	o		x	x					o
	f		x	x		o	o					o
5:14	cd	x	x	x	o							o
	e				o	x	x	x	x	x	x	o
	f		x	x	o							o
5:16	a				o			x	x	x	x	o
5:18	a	o	o	o	o	x	x	x	x	x	x	o
	b	x	x	x	o	o	o	o	o	o	o	o
	c	x	x	x	o							o
6:1	a				o			x	x	x	x	o
6:3	a				o	x	x	x	x	x	x	o
	c		x	x	o							o
6:4	ab		x	x	o	x		x	x	x	x	o
	c				o			x	x	x	x	o
	d		x	x	o							o
	g				o			x	x	x	x	o
	h	x	x	x	o							o
6:5	a		x	x	o							o
6:6	a				o	x	x	x	x	x	x	o
	b				o			x	x		x	o

44   Psalms of Solomon

		253	655	659	336	629	769	149	260	471	606	3004
7:1	a		*	x	o							o
	b		x	x	o							o
	c				o	x	x	x	x	x	x	o
7:3	a		x	x	o							o
	b		x	x	o							o
7:4	a		x	x	o							o
7:7	a				o	x	x					o
	b				o	x	x					o
7:8	c		c	x	o							o
7:9	b		x	x	o	o	o					o
7:10	a	x	x	x	o							o
8:2	b		x	x	o							o
	c				o	x	x					o
8:3	a				o	x	x	x	x	x	x	o
	c		x	x	o							o
	d				o	x	x					o
8:4					o			x	x	x	x	o
8:6	a				o	x	x	x	x	x	x	o
	d	x	x	x	o							o
8:7	b		x	x	o							o
8:8	ab	x	x	x	o							o
	d				o	x	x					o
8:9	a		x	x	o							o
	c				o	x	x					o
	d				o	x	x					o
8:10	a				o	x	x	x	x	x	x	o
8:11	a				o	x	x	x	x	x	x	o
	c				o	x	x	x	x	x	x	o
8:12	a				o	x	x	x	x	x	x	o
	f		x	x								o
	g				x	x	x	x	x	x	x	o
8:14	a		x	x								o
	b							x	x		x	o
8:16	d				x	o	x	x	x		x	o
	f				x	x		x	x	x	x	o
8:17	d					o		x	x	x	x	o
8:19	a		x	x								o
	b				x	x	x	x	x	x	x	o
	c		x	x								o
8:20	a		x	x								o
	b				x	x	x	x	x	x	x	o
8:21	b				x	x	x	x	x	x	x	o
8:22	d	x	x	x								o
8:24	a		*	x								o
8:25	a		x	x								o
	b				x	x	x	x	x	x	x	o
	c							x	x	x	x	o
8:26	a	x	x	x								o
8:28	bc				x	x	x	x	x	x	x	o
	d	x	x	x								o
8:29	b		x	x								o
	c	x	x	x								o
8:30	b				x	x	x	x	x	x	x	o
	c				x	x	x	x	x	x	x	o
8:31					x	x	x	x	x	x	x	o

Manuscript Groupings   45

		253	655	659	336	629	769	149	260	471	606	3004
8:32	a		x	x								o
	b	x	x	x								o
8:33	a					x	x					o
	c				x	x	x					o
8:34	b							x	x	x	x	o
9:1	b		x	x								o
	d							x	x	x	x	o
	f		x	x								o
	i		x	x								o
9:2	b							x	x	x	x	o
	c	x		x								o
9:3	d				x	x	x	x	x	x	x	o
9:4	a	x	x	x	x							o
	c		x	x								o
9:5	a		x	x								o
	b				x	x	x	x	x	x	x	o
	c							x	x	x	x	o
9:6	f	o	o	o	o	x	x	x	x	x	x	o
	h	o	x	x	o	o	o	o	o	o	o	o
9:7	e		x	x								o
	f				x	x	x	x	x	x	x	o
9:8	c	x	x	x								o
	e				x	x	x	x	x	x	x	o
	i				x	x	x	x	x	x	x	o
9:9	bd				x	x	x	x	x	x	x	o
	ce	x	x	x								o
	f	x	x	*								o
9:10			x	x								o
9:11	a	x	x	x		x						o
	d		x	x								o
10.1	c		x	x								o
	d				x	x	x	x	x	x	x	o
10:2	a	x	x	x								o
	c		x	x	o	o						o
	d		o	o	x	x						o
10:3	ab	x	x	x								o
10:4	a	x	x	x								o
	b		x	x								o
	c							x	x	x	x	o
	d		x	x								o
10:5	b	x	x									o
	f							x	x	x	x	o
10:7	a				o	x	x	x	x	x	x	o
10:8	a		x	x								o
	b		x	x								o
	cd	x	x	x				x	x	x	x	o
11:1	b			x			x					o
	c							x	x	x	x	o
11:2	c	x	x	x								o
11:4	b				x	x	x	x	x	x	x	o
11:5	a		x	x								o
	d									x	x	o
11:7	a		x	x								o
	e					x	x					o
	g					c	x					o

46   Psalms of Solomon

		253	655	659	336	629	769	149	260	471	606	3004
11:8								x	x	x	x	o
12:2	a		o	o				x	x	x	x	o
	b		x	*				o	o	o	o	o
	d					o	o	x	x	x	x	o
	e					x	x	o	o	o	o	o
	gh							x	x	x	x	o
	j							x	x	x	x	o
12:3	c				x			x	x	x	x	o
	d	o	o	o	o	o	o	x	x	x	x	o
	e	x	x	x	o	o	o	o	o	o	o	o
	f	o	o	o	x	x	x	o	o	o	x	o
12:4	c				x	x	x	x	x	x	x	o
12:5	a	x	x	x								o
	b	x	x	x								o
	c	x	x	x								o
	d	x	x	x								o
12:6	c		x	x								o
	e		o	o	x		x					o
	f		x	x								o
	g				x	x	x	x	x	x	x	o
	k	x	x	x								o
13:2	b		x	x			o					o
13:3	a		o	o	x	o		x	x	x	x	o
	de				x	x		x	x	x	x	o
	g							x	x	x	x	o
13:4					x	x						o
13:5	c	x	x	x								o
13:6	b				x	x	x			x	x	o
	c					x	x					o
	d				x	x	x	x	x	x	x	o
	f				x			x	x	x	x	o
13:7	a					x	x					o
	c	x	x	x		o	o					o
13:11	c	x		x								o
13:12		x	x	x								o
14:2	b	o	o	o	o			x	x	x	x	o
	d	x	x	x	o			o	o	o	o	o
14:3	c		c	c								o
	d				x	x	x	x	x	x	x	o
	e		x	x								o
14:5	b		x	x	x			x	x	x	x	o
	c							x	x	x	x	o
14:7								x	x	x	x	o
14:8	a		x	x								o
	b					x	x					o
	c	x	x	x								o
14:9	b		x	x								o
	c				x	x	x	x	x	x	x	o
15:1	b		x	x								o
	d	x	x	c								o
15:2	d		x	x								o
	e		x	x								o
15:3	d		x	x								o
15:4	b					x	*					o
	c	x	x	x								o

Manuscript Groupings   47

		253	655	659	336	629	769	149	260	471	606	3004
15:7	a				x	x	x	x	x	x	x	o
	b	x	x	x		x	x	x	x	x	x	o
	c	x	x	x								o
	f					x	x	x				o
15:8	a					x	x	x	x	x	x	o
	b		x	x								o
	e		o	o	x	x	x	x	x	x	x	o
	fg		x	x	o	o	o	o	o	o	o	o
	i					x	x					o
15:9	a	c	x	x		o		x	x	x	x	o
15:10	b	x	x	x								o
15:11	a		x	x								o
	b		x	x								o
	d				x	x	x	x	x	x	x	o
	f	o	x	x								o
15:12	a							x	x	x	x	o
	b		x	x								o
	c		x	x								o
	d							x	x	x	x	o
15:13	b							x	x	x	x	o
	cd[49]				x	x	x					o
16:1	h					x	x			o		o
	i				x	x	x	x	x	x		o
16:2			x	x								o
16:3	a		x	x								o
16:5	c		x	x								o
	d	x	x	x								o
16:6	b	x	x	x								o
	c		x	x								o
	d	x	x	x								o
16:8	b		x	x								o
16:12	a					o	o	x	x	x	x	o
16:13	a					o		x	x	x	x	o
16:14	a		x	x		o						o
	b					o	x	x	x	x	x	o
17:1	b	x	x	x		o						o
	d	x	x	x		o						o
17:3	a		x	x		o						o
	c[50]				x	o		x	x	x	x	
	d[51]					o	x					x
	e				x	o	x	x	x	x	x	x
	f	x	x	x		o						
17:4	c	x	x	x		o						
17:5	c	x	x	x		o				o		
	i				x	o	x	x	x	x	x	x
17:6	b				x	o						x
	d					o		x	x	x	x	x
17:7		x	x	x		o						
17:8	b					o		x	x	x	x	x
17:9	a					o		x	x	x	x	x
	d					o		x	x	x	x	x
17:10	c		x	x		o						
17:11	f				x	o						x
17:13	b	x	x	x		o						
17:14	a		x	x		o						

48   Psalms of Solomon

		253	655	659	336	629	769	149	260	471	606	3004
17:15	a				o	o	x	x	x	x	x	x
	d	o	o	o	x	o	x	x	x	x	x	x
	e	x	x	x	o	o	o	o	o	o	o	o
17:16	a				x	o	x	x	x	x	x	x
	d		x	x		o						
17:17	a		x	x		o						
	b		x	x		o						
	c	x	x	x		o						
18:18	a	x	x	x		o						
	d		x	x		o						
17:19	b		x	x		o						
17:20	c		x	x		o						
17:21	b		x	x		o						
	e	o	o	o	o	o	o	x	x	o	o	o
	f	x	o	x	o	o	o	o	o	o	o	o
	g	o	o	o	o	o	o	o	o	x	x	x
17:22	e		x	x		o						
17:23	b		o	o	x	o	x					
	c		x	x	o	o	o					
	d		x	x		o						
	f				o	o		x	x		x	x
17:25	a					o				x		*
17:26			x	x		o						
17:27	a	x	x	x		o						
	c		x	x		o						
	de				x	o	x	x	x	x	x	x
17:28	b		x	x		o						
17:29						o				x		*
17:30	a		x	x		o						
	c		x	x	x	o	x	x	x	x	x	x
	d		o	o	x	o		x	x	x	x	x
	e		x	x	o	o		o	o	o	o	o
17:32	c		x	x		o						
17:33	c		x	x		o						
	d				x	o	x	x	x	x	x	x
17:34	b	x	x	x		o						
17:35	a	x	x	x	x	o						
17:36	a		x	x		o						
	b	x	x	x		o						
17:37	f	x	*	x		o						
17:40	a		x	x		o						
	b		x	x		o						
	f		x	x		o						
17:41	a		x	x		o						
	b					o	*	x	x	x	x	x
	d		*	*		o					o	
17:43	a				x	o	x	x	x	x	x	x
	d				x	o	x	x	x	x	x	x
	e					o		x	x	x	x	x
	fg	x	x	x		o						
17:44	a				x	o	x	x	x	x	c	x
	d	x	x	x	x	o	x					
	e	x	x	x		o						
17:46			x	x		o						
18:1	a	x	x	x		o						

Manuscript Groupings   49

		253	655	659	336	629	769	149	260	471	606	3004
18:2	b		x	x		o						
	c		x	x		o						
18:3	a				x	o	x	x	x	x	x	x
	b		x	x		o						
18:4	e					o		x	x	x	x	x
18:5	a	x	x	x	o	o						
	b		o	o	o	o		x	x	x	x	x
	c		x	x	o	o						
18:6	a				o	o		x	x	x	x	x
	b	x	x	x	o	o						
18:7	b		x	x	o	o						
18:8	a	x	x	x	o	o						
	b				o	o		x	x	x	x	x
18:9	a				o	o	x	x	x	x	x	x
	b	x	x	x	o	o		x	x	o		o
	c	o	o	o	o	o		o	o	x		*
18:10	a				o	o	x	x	x	x	x	x
18:12	a				o	o	x	x	x	x	x	x

THE MANUSCRIPT GROUPINGS

There are two criteria for defining a text group according to the CPM. The first is internal consistency. MSS of an alleged group must have some readings where two-thirds of the witnesses agree.[52] Four of von Soden's text groups for Luke were rejected by Wisse because this cohesion was lacking.[53] A second criterion for the definition of a group is that the profile of an alleged group must differ significantly from the profiles of other groups. There must be at least two test readings per chapter at which allegedly different groups differ.[54] It is not necessary that a group display unique readings. In the application of the CPM to Luke 1, group K^1 contained the readings numbered 6, 8, 22, 34, and 52, while K^x read the readings 6, 9, 34, and 36. Although two readings were shared between the groups, the groups differed at five other places and thus qualified as distinct text groups.[55]

Von Gebhardt's groups exceed the requirements of the criterion of internal consistency. MSS 629-769 agree in eighty-five test readings, and differ in eleven readings.[56] The members of the 260 group all agree in 156 test readings, and differ in only twenty-two readings.[57] The criterion of significant difference between groups is also satisfied: for those chapters in which 629 has no major omissions, no fewer than two test readings separate the 629 group from the 260 group.[58] The CPM has therefore confirmed the existence of these text groupings.[59]

In the profile above, MSS 655 and 659 were tentatively grouped with 253 on the basis of the observed frequency of common readings. The identification of these MSS as a text group can now be confirmed by the CPM. According to the CPM, a group may be identified both by its agreements with the base text and by its common agreements against that base.[60] Since the collation base used in the present work most closely resembles the text of 253, the group relationships of this MS can be seen most clearly by observing its points of agreement with the base. These points appear as blanks in the profile.[61] MSS 253, 655, and 659 agree against the base in ninety-nine readings and agree with the base in 175 readings. There are therefore 274 readings at which 253, 655, and 659 agree. There are 159 test readings where these MSS do not agree. The greatest number of these are instances where 655 and 659 agree together against 253. While these three witnesses display less internal consistency than the members of the 260 group, they are still within the limits to qualify as a text group. The criterion of significant difference between groups is also satisfied by 253-655-659: there are only seven test readings where a majority of 253-655-659 agrees with a reading of 149-260-471-606.[62] In the sections of the $PsSol$ where the text of 629 is complete, there are only three test readings where a majority of the 253 group agrees with 629 and 769.[63] The CPM has therefore identified the existence of 253-655-659 as a text group for the $PsSol$ in addition to the two groups which were identified by von Gebhardt.

MS 336 cannot be classified as a member of any text group of the $PsSol$. While this MS shares many readings with both the 260 and 629 groups, in the majority of cases these are readings where both of the latter agree against the 253 group. These readings therefore represent peculiarities of the 253 group, and cannot be used to classify 336. In the portions of the $PsSol$ where 336 and 629 are complete, 336 shares only one test reading exclusively with the 253 group,[64] four readings exclusively with the 629 group,[65] and seven readings exclusively with the 260 group.[66] Each of these is much less than the

Manuscript Groupings   51

internal consistency displayed among the members of the known groups. While 336 is a single MS, its profile is more characteristic of a distinct text type than of a member of any group. This witness must therefore be considered to be a singular MS, without membership in any group of extant MSS of the *PsaSol*.[67]

Among the uses for which the CPM was developed was that of rapidly identifying a MS in terms of its group membership. This is accomplished by comparing its readings with the characteristic test readings of all known groups.[68] When the readings of 3004 are compared with the group test readings for that portion of the *PsaSol*, MS 3004 is seen to share no test readings with the 253 group. Sixteen of the remaining test readings are instances where all other groups agree against the 253 text group, and must be excluded.[69] MS 3004 shares three of the remaining eight test readings for 336 and one of the four test readings for 769.[70] Of the twelve remaining test readings for the 260 group, all but one is read by 3004.[71] This MS is therefore identified as a member of the 260 group. Within this group, 3004 has the closest affinities to 471: the original text of 3004 follows 471 four times in departing from the text of 260.[72]

The following text groups have been identified by the CPM: the 253 group, consisting of 253, 655, and 659; the 260 group, consisting of 149, 260, 471, 606, and 3004; the singular MS 336; and the 629 group, consisting of 629 and 769. The characteristic readings of the component witnesses of the text groups will be examined in the following chapter, and the relationship among the witnesses will be established.

CHAPTER FOUR
TEXTUAL CHARACTERISTICS OF THE MANUSCRIPTS

The Claremont Profile Method was employed in the preceding chapter to confirm the existence of the *Pssol* text groups which had been identified by von Gebhardt and to classify the witnesses which he had not examined. The following text types were established: the 253 group, consisting of 253, 655, and 659; the 260 group, consisting of 149, 260, 471, 606, and 3004; the singular witness 336; and the 629 group, consisting of 629 and 769.

The task of examining the relationship among the various MSS, however, is not completed simply by establishing the fact of the several text groupings. While the procedures of the CPM allow a rapid classification of the witnesses into text groups, the nature of the relationships among the MSS can only be determined by a detailed examination of their readings.[1] This is in accord with the text-critical maxim that witnesses are not to be counted, but weighed.

The present and following chapters will undertake an examination of the characteristic readings of the MSS and text groups. This examination will have two objectives. The first objective is phenomenological: to describe the textual characteristics of the witnesses and text types. The second objective is analytical: to observe those readings which offer evidence of the relationships among the MSS and groups and so to determine the history of their textual transmissions. The descriptive portion of this undertaking will be found in the present and following chapters. The determination of the relationships among the constituent MSS of the text groups will be found in the present chapter; the determination of the relationships among the groups and a reconstruction of the whole textual tradition will be found in chapter six. Since, however, the present chapter will reconstruct the genealogical relationships within each text group, it may be useful to introduce below the stemma of the entire MS tradition which will be demonstrated in chapter six, so that this may be kept in mind during the discussion which follows:

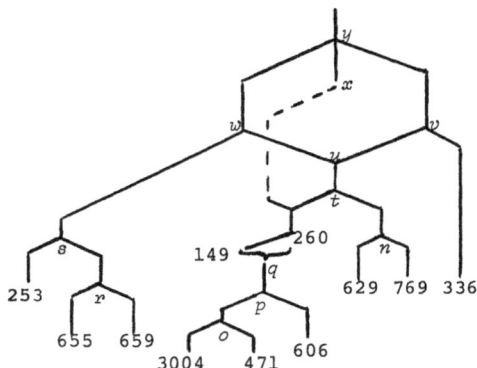

Since the description of the textual characteristics of the witnesses and text groups is intended to be a contribution in its own right to the study of the *PsSol*, not all of the data which will be presented in the present and following chapters will be utilized in analyzing the relationships among the MSS and groups. The component MSS of the 253, 260 and 629 text groups will be examined in the present chapter, in part to determine which MSS best represent the text of each group; since 336 is a singular witness of a distinct text type, its textual characteristics will be examined in chapter five.[2]

METHOD OF PROCEDURE

The large quantity of variant readings in the eighteen *PsSol* has made it impractical to examine every variation contained in every witness of each text group. For this reason, the following studies have been limited to those variations at which one MS reads differently from the reading of the majority of its group, either with or against the base text. This limitation will reduce the quantity of variant readings to be examined. In addition, this procedure provides a greater probability that the significant relationships within the groups may be discovered, since a reading where no MSS of a group agree may

Manuscript Characteristics   55

represent a case where the original reading has been lost.³
Since, however, the 629 group has only two members, the examination will include all readings where these MSS differ. MSS
149 and 260 of the 260 group will be treated as one witness,
since their readings are, with one exception, identical.⁴ Since
3004 contains only a fragment of text, its readings will be compared with those of 149-260 separately.

The following procedure was followed in identifying
characteristic readings: Lists were made of the readings where
each MS differed from the majority of the MSS of its text group.
The character of the variation at each point was classified,
using the categories used by McReynolds in describing the CPM
test readings. These categories are verb changes, transpositions, omissions, additions, substitutions, case changes, and
spelling changes.⁵ The classifications for each witness were
examined and, where practical, were further analyzed in terms
of the specific nature of the variant readings. A more narrowly
defined initial list of characteristics was produced for each
MS. For example, the spelling changes between 253 and 655-659
were further categorized as itacisms, exchanges between *alpha*
and *epsilon* and between *alpha iota* and *epsilon*, variations in
the length of the *e*-vowel and of the *o*-vowel, changes involving
the omission of letters, and the presence or absence of the
final *nu* or *sigma*.

In order to avoid classifying random variations as textual
characteristics, it is necessary to establish a working definition of a "textual characteristic." The following was adopted
for the purposes of the present work: For a witness with fewer
than one hundred variant readings, a specific kind of variation
must occur twice to be considered to be a textual characteristic; for a witness with one hundred or more variations, there
must be examples of the specific kind of variation amounting to
two percent of the total number of variant readings. The
establishment of two as the minimum number of variants ensures,
in the case of a MS with a small number of variations, that no
variation could be considered to be characteristic of a witness
on the basis of only one occurrence. In the case of a MS with
a larger number of variations, the minimum requirement of two
percent ensures that a specific kind of variant must occur in

all witnesses in roughly the same proportions in order to qualify as a textual characteristic. Since only thirty-five variants were examined at which 659 differed from 253-655, any category of variant readings must have at least two examples to be considered to be characteristic of 659. On the other hand, there are 237 instances where 253 differs from 655-659. For a category of variant readings to be recognized as a textual characteristic of 253, therefore, there must be at least five examples of that category. Since, for example, there are only three variations involving the use of the final *sigma*, these variations cannot qualify as a textual characteristic of 253.

Since one of the objectives of the present and following chapters is to describe the textual characteristics of the MSS and groups, no attempt will be made to analyze the significance of all of the variant readings. Some, such as itacisms, will be noted without attempting to describe which reading is original. Where, however, an earlier stage of the textual tradition can be identified on the basis of the readings, this will be observed and will be used as evidence for determining the nature of the relationships among the witnesses and text types and for reconstructing the history of the transmission and the text.

In order to avoid lengthy circumlocutions, terms such as "added," "omitted", and "substituted" will be used throughout these chapters to refer to the presence or absence of readings as the MSS are contrasted to each other. Except where the contrary is stated or clearly implied, the use of these terms relates to the description of the readings of the MSS, and not to the history of their textual transmission. It should not be inferred, therefore, that the use of the term "added" implies the judgement of the author that the reading so described was absent from an earlier stage in the history of the text.[6]

The textual characteristics of the component witnesses of the *PssSol* text groups will be examined on the following pages. Variant readings are cited by chapter, verse, and, by lower case letters, the specific variation within each verse. Thus, 4:23c refers to the third variant in the collation at 4:23. Where reference is made to more than one reading in the

Manuscript Characteristics   57

same verse, the letters may be combined, as: 13:2ac. Economy
of space forbids reproducing each reading to be referred to in
the present work. By means of this system of designation, the
readings may be readily located in the collation.

THE 253 GROUP

Readings where 253 differs from 655-659.

There are 237 points in the text of the *PssSol* where 253
differs from 655 and 659. The majority of the characteristic
readings of MS 253 are spelling variations.[7] Itacism occurs
forty-one times. At 4:23c, the first person plural pronoun
ημας is read in place of the second person υμας found in 655-
659.[8] παιδεια in 253 is characteristically spelled παιδια in
655-659.[9] Exchanges between *alpha* and *epsilon* occur ten
times.[10] Although this exchange normally produces only a spelling variation, as in 2:11de and in 4:16ce, an apparent grammatical alteration may also result: at 17:27c the reading
παντας in 655-659 alters the case from nominative to accusative.
There are six instances of variation in the length of the *e*-
vowel.[11] The most common is the exchange between *epsilon* and
eta, occurring three times.[12] MS 253 reads ηυλογησεν at 6:4a,
a spelling characteristic of Sinaiticus and Alexandrinus. The
past tenses of ευλογεω do not normally show the augment.[13]
There are ten cases of variation in the length of the *o*-vowel,
a common scribal variation.[14] There are ten instances of variation between 253 and 655-659 with regard to the use of the
final *nu*.[15] In all but two instances, 8:2a and 8:7c, the *nu*
is read by 253 and omitted by 655-659. The omission of the
final *nu* is a characteristic of later MSS.[16] MS 253 preserves
an earlier form of the text. Finally, there are five instances
where an infinitive read by 253 appears in 655-659 as a participle or a finite verb. In each of these cases, however, the
change is between a form terminating in *alpha iota* and forms
ending in *alpha sigma* or *alpha nu*.[17] These instances have been
classified as spelling variations rather than as grammatical
changes.

A smaller number of the variations between 253 and 655-659 are changes in wording or of grammar. There are twenty-two cases of omission or addition. Of these, fifteen readings omitted from 655-659 occur in 253. Six of these are cases of haplography in 655-659, in which 253 has preserved the original reading.[18] Dittography has occurred once in 253: the words την γην και η δοξα αυτων εως εσχατου are repeated at 1:4d. There are eight other instances where a reading of 253 is not found in 655-659.[19] There are eight readings at which 253 does not read material found in 655-659. Two of these are the result of dittography in 655-659; 253 preserves the original reading.[20]

Exclusive of spelling errors and nonsense readings, there are fifteen instances of substitution between 253 and 655-659.[21] Examples include the substitution of Ισραηλ for Ιερουσαλημ by 253 at 2:22f, the reading κυριον for θεον by 655-659 at 4:21b, and the use of πλανη for πλανησει by 655-659 at 8:19c.[22] The latter was made in the interest of a more intelligible text. In the majority of substitutions between 253 and 655-659, the readings of the latter are unique to these MSS.[23] There are five instances of change in number between 253 and 655-659.[24] In each of these cases, the readings of 655-659 are shared by no other witnesses.

Readings where 655 differs from 253-659.

There are twenty-two places where the text of 655 differs from that of 253-659. With two exceptions, these readings are all spelling changes or instances of erroneous omissions or additions by dittography.

Itacism occurs ten times. Examples include the misspelling of diphthongs such as εη for ει at 9:7d and οσιοει for οσιοι at 14:3b.[25] In these two instances it is difficult to avoid the impression that the scribe had sounded out each letter of the diphthong separately.

There are two cases of omission in 655. At 17:13c the preposition εν, read by the other members of the group and by 336, and normally found before the dative case, is omitted. At 17:15c the noun υιοι, read by all other MSS, is omitted from 655.

Manuscript Characteristics   59

There are three instances of dittography. At 9:11 the
words εις τον αιωνα και ετι appear in 655 as εις τον αιωνα και
εις τον αιωνα του αιωνος. At 15:2g the words τη αληθεια are
repeated from the previous line. At 17:5h the word μετα, found
at the bottom of the page in the MS, is repeated at the top of
the following page.

There are two additions. At 15:8d the letters ωκομενου
are found in the text preceding αμαρτωλους. This may have been
a scribal error for ωκυδρομενους.[26] At 17:11d επι appears
before την γην.

Readings where 659 differs from 253-655.

In thirty-five cases the text of 659 differs from that of
253-655. The majority of these are spelling changes.

Itacism occurs six times. Examples are παρασιωπησεις for
παρασιωπησης at 5:2b, φησεται for φεισεται at 13:10b, and
βασιλιον for βασιλειον at 17:4f.[27]

The final *nu* is omitted at 10:2e υπομενουσι and in the
original reading at 17:31g αυτη. A *sigma* has been omitted from
the ends of two words: ημει at 8:29a and μερι at 14:5a. At
11:7b the *alpha* is missing from the end of ιματια, and at 8:33d
the last two syllables do not appear in σαλευθησομεθα. One of
a pair of doubled *lambdas* is missing from συναλλαγματι at 4:4b.
At 4:15g the *iota* is missing from the diphthong *alpha iota* in
απoριαις. An *eta* has been omitted from εξησθενηκοτας at 17:31d,
and another *eta* in the same word has been changed to an *omicron*.
Each of these represent alterations of the original readings.

There are two instances of confusion between a *pi* and a
tau. At 10:3b διαπρεψει in 253-655 is read as διατρεψει. At
13:3f επιλλοσαν is read by 659 in place of ετιλλοσαν.

In three readings an *eta* or *epsilon iota* appears in 659
as the shorter vowel *epsilon*: υπεριδες at 8:30a, ελεησεν at
11:1b, and ες for εις at 17:33g. The length of the *o*-vowel has
been changed four times. In three instances an *omicron* has
been lengthened to an *omega*: 11:5e, 14:9a, and 17:31c. At
8:23b the *omega* of αυτων has been shortened to an *omicron*.

On three occasions 659 includes material not found in 253-655. The articles το and ο are read at 9:8h and 11:6, respectively. The conjunction και is found at 5:5b. Each of these are probable scribal emendations in the interest of a smoother text.[28]

There are two omissions by haplography in 659. At 16:12c, εν τω ενισχυσαι σε την ψυχην μου is omitted, as are the words πρημωσεν ο ανεμος την γην at 17:11a. An additional omission is that of και at 17:40a.

Characteristics of the manuscripts of the 253 group.

It is useful to summarize the findings of the previous pages. When compared with the other members of its text group, 253 is characterized by itacism, variations between *alpha* and *epsilon*, variations in the length of the *e*- and *o*-vowels, and by the presence of the final *nu*. Haplography, substitutions, and changes in number are shared by 655 and 659. MS 655 is characterized by itacism and other spelling errors, and by omissions and dittography. MS 659 is characterized by spelling errors, haplography, and several attempts to produce a smoother text.

In order to work out the relationship among these witnesses it is useful to recall that 253 is a parchment codex from the eleventh or twelfth century, and that 655 and 659 are paper codices, written by the same scribe in the sixteenth century. In addition to the dates which have been assigned to the witnesses and the differences in writing materials,[29] there are several reasons for concluding that 253 represents a text closer to the archetype of the 253 group: the presence of the final *nu*, found eight times in 253, is a characteristic of earlier MSS.[30] The substitution of πλανη for πλανησει by 655-659 at 8:19c is the replacement of an uncommon term by one more familiar. Alterations of this nature are characteristic of later stages in the transmission of a text.

In the comparison of the readings of 253 and 655-659, a total of eighteen readings were observed at which the 253 text may be identified as more probably original or preserving a more ancient form of the text. These readings include the use

Manuscript Characteristics   61

of the archaic final *nu* and the preservation of the relatively
uncommon term at 8:19c, and instances of haplography and dittography in 655-659, at which the latter have departed from the
received text. In only one reading of 253, the dittography at
1:4d, has that MS departed from a text preserved by 655-659.
By contrast, when 655 has been compared to 253-659, five readings may be identified, on the basis of spelling and haplography, where 655 has departed from its received text. Fourteen such readings may be identified, on the basis of spelling,
scribal additions, and haplography, in 659. The general
deterioration of the readings of 655-659 when compared to those
of 253 indicates that these represent a later stage in the
textual tradition.

The fact that 655 and 659 were written by the same copyist, together with the high number of readings shared by the
two witnesses, indicates that these MSS were both copied from
the same exemplar. It is not possible that one of these MSS
was copied from the other, since each preserves a number of
readings not found in the other.[31]

The exemplar of 655-659 could not have been 253, since
these two MSS share a number of readings which are not read by
253. It is this exemplar which substituted κυριον for θεον at
4:21b and πλανη for πλανησει at 8:19c, and produced the other
readings shared by 655 and 659 against 253.

In addition, the evidence indicates that the exemplar of
655-659 was not a direct or indirect copy of 253. At 1:4d 253
adds by dittography: την γην και η δοξα αυτων εως εσχατου.
These words do not appear in 655-659 or in any other MSS. At
2:22f 253 reads Ισραηλ for Ιερουσαλημ, the reading of all other
witnesses. It is unlikely that in these instances the exemplar
of 655-659 has altered the readings of 253. This is especially
true with regard to the substitution at 2:22f. Had the exemplar of 655-659 been copying from 253, there is nothing in this
reading which would have prompted him to have introduced a
change in the text.[32]

One might be tempted to offer the hypothesis that the
exemplar of 655-659 was descended from the text of 253, but
that the text has been corrected on the basis of other witnesses: at 1:4a and 14:5b the readings of 655-659 against

253 are also read by the members of the 260 group. Such a hypothesis would account for these readings and those described in the preceding paragraph on the basis of textual mixture introduced by corrections from a different tradition. This conclusion, however is not warranted by the evidence. The reading at 14:5b is the addition of the article η. The preceding noun in the text has this article in all MSS, and a concern for parallel form may have induced separate scribes to have supplied the article before the following word as well.[33] The case at 1:4a is the variation between διεδοθη, read by 253, 336, and 769, and διελθου, read by 655-659 and the 260 group.[34] It has already been observed by von Gebhardt, however, that these differ by the letters *delta* and *lambda* and *theta* and *omicron*.[35] The uncial forms of each of these pairs of letters are similar. The apparent difference between ΔΙΕΔΟΘΗ and ΔΙΕΛΘΟΙ has been produced by scribal error, and does not indicate a dependence of 655-659 on the 260 group. Furthermore, had the 260 text been available to correct the exemplar of 655-659 at these points, it would also have been available for correcting the text at other points. The fact that few parallels exist between the readings of 655-659 and the other witnesses is the strongest evidence that no such corrections took place.

Most of the readings of 655 and 659 support the observation that the scribe responsible for these MSS was not a highly skilled copyist. Both MSS exhibit frequent errors in their departures from their common exemplar. Running counter to this observation, however, are the instances where each MS preserves readings which cannot be attributed to an illiterate or unskilled scribe. Examples of these readings are 15:8d and 17:11d in 655 and 9:8h, 11:6, and 5:5b in 659. Each of these represents a scribal attempt to improve the reading, and, in spite of appearing to be characteristic readings of the separate MSS, should probably be viewed as changes introduced by the exemplar of 655-659, but which were retained in only one or the other MS due to scribal error by the copyist of 655 and 659.

On the basis of the foregoing, the exemplar of 655-659 may now be described in the following manner. This MS represents a text which descended from an uncial MS closely

Manuscript Characteristics 63

resembling the present MS 253. Although this exemplar included many scribal errors, it has also preserved original group readings from which 253 had departed at 1:4d and 2:22f. At several points this text attempted to improve upon the readings of its tradition. These include the instances cited in the previous paragraph and the readings at 4:21b, 8:19c, 8:20a, and 9:1b.

The relationship among the witnesses of the 253 group may be represented in graphic form as follows:

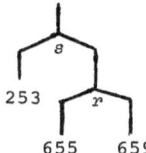

The common archetype, from which all members of the 253 group are descended, appears in this stemma as an s. The common exemplar behind 655 and 659 is represented by an r.

THE 260 GROUP

There are fewer textual variations separating the witnesses of the 260 group than were found among the MSS of the 253 group. It will be recalled that there were 237 instances where the text of 253 differs from that of 655-659. By contrast, the witness which differs the most often from the other members of the 260 group, MS 471, does so only forty-six times.[36]

The relationship of 149 to 260.

The texts of 149 and 260 are identical with the exception of the reading at 16:13a, where there has been a correction in each MS. All non-260 group MSS preserve the following word order: παιδειαν εν πενια.[37] MS 149 has changed the word order, but has indicated the correct order by the letters *alpha* and *beta* above the text. The text appears as: ἐν πενια$^\beta$ παιδειαν$^\alpha$. MS 260 has the same word order as 149 and indicates the correct order in the same manner. In addition, however, the εν is written above πενια and a gap appears between πενια and παιδειαν. The text appears to have originally been written πενια εν παιδειαν, and then to have been corrected by erasing the εν and adding it above πενια. The text of 260 therefore appears as the following: $\overset{\beta}{\overset{\nu}{\pi}}$ενια .. $\overset{\alpha}{\pi}$αιδειαν. The other MSS of the 260 group read εν πενια παιδειαν, without any indication of the correct word order.[38]

The only evidence for the relationship between 149 and 260 is the position of the εν in both MSS. The *alpha* and *beta* indicate that the exemplar read παιδειαν εν πενια, together with all non-360 group witnesses. Two explanations are possible for the difference between 149 and 260. If 149 had transposed παιδειαν and εν πενια, and had been corrected by the addition of the *alpha* and *beta*, an additional error would have to have been committed by 260 to have produced the dislocation of the εν. If, on the other hand, 260 had originally read πενια εν παιδειαν, and had been corrected by relocating the εν and by adding the small letters to indicate the correct word order, the reading of 149 could have been produced from this if the scribe had observed the correction of the εν, but had initially overlooked or had misunderstood the significance of the *alpha* and *beta*. This solution explains the readings of 149 and 260 more satisfactorily since the scribe of 149, having directed his attention to locating the εν correctly in the text, may well have been distracted from observing the small letters which 260 had added. MS 260 is therefore to be identified as the ememplar from which 149 has been made.[39]

Readings where 149-260 differ from 471-606.

Since the readings of 149-260 are, with the exception noted in the preceding paragraphs, identical, they may be treated as representing a common text. There are ten instances where 149-260 differ from 471-606. These are most frequently spelling changes. Itacism occurs at 6:4e. *Alpha* and *epsilon* are exchanged at 2:22h and 17:21eg. The contraction αλλ' is spelled in full by 149-260 at 5:7b. An omission of a final *nu*, a characteristic of later MSS,[40] has occurred in 471-606

Manuscript Groupings   65

at 1:5c. The latter witnesses read the indicative αποπεσει at 4:16b, while 149-260 read the optative αποπεσοι. The preceding verb is optative in all MSS.[41] Since, in the interest of parallel usage, a later scribe would most likely have retained the optative of 149-260, this change should be understood as a spelling rather than as a grammatical alteration.

There are two variations in number and case between 149-260 and 471-606. At 4:15b the plural noun απορίαις is read as singular by 471-606. At 5:1b the dative τω ονοματι of 149-260 is read as the accusative το ονομα by 471-606. While either case is possible following the verb αινεω,[42] the use of the accusative is the prevailing practice of the LXX.[43] The text of the later MSS 471 and 606 has been conformed to Septuagintal usage.

There are two instances of change in wording between 149-260 and 471-606. At 11:5d the verb εσκιασαν of 149-260 is changed to εσκιρτησαν by 471-606, apparently under the influence of Wis 17:18.[44] At 13:6b the article η is omitted by 471-606, perhaps by assimilation to the final vowel of the preceding word δεινη.

Readings where 471 differs from 149-260-606.

Readings of 471 differ from the other members of the 260 group forty-five times. The largest number of variant readings in 471 are omissions of an initial letter. This has occurred twenty-nine times.[45] There are four other instances of the omission of letters in this MS: 2:23c, 8:10a, 9:1e, and 17:23a.

Five other spelling variations appear in 471. The diphthong *alpha iota* appears in place of an *epsilon* at 8:12e. A *sigma* is substituted for a *nu* at the end of ωνειδισαν, at 2:19c.[46] Other spelling variations have occurred at 17:5d, 17:8a, and 17:13c.

Several variant readings of 471 involve a change in wording. The articles ο and η are omitted at 9:6c and 13:6b, respectively. At 17:25a the words εν απειλη αυτου φυγειν εθνη απο προσωπου αυτου are omitted by haplography. The διαψαλμα is missing at 17:29 and 18:9c.[47] In the interest of producing a smoother text, a καυ has been added at 2:29d. At 6:6b the second declension masculine accusative ελεον, read by other members of the 260 group, has been replaced by the third declension neuter ελεος. The latter is more common in both the NT and the LXX, and is what a scribe would have preferred.[48]

Readings where 606 differs from 149-260-471.

There are eleven instances where the text of 606 differs from the readings of 149-260-471. Several of these are obvious spelling changes. The final *nu* has been omitted at 2:11c. At 8:28c the spelling ελαυου has been produced by an exchange of an *epsilon* and an *alpha iota*. At 12:2h an additional *lambda* has been added, producing the spelling αλλω. At 16:1i the *theta* has been omitted from καταφθορα. There are several additional spelling variations which have resulted in apparent changes in wording. At 12:4b κακων is read in place of ακακων. At 16:12d 606 reads ισχυσαι for ενισχυσαι. Αυξει appears in place of αξει at 17:41c. The first two of these represent the omission of an *alpha* and of the previx εν-, respectively. The reading at 17:41c is caused by the addition of an *upsilon* following the initial *alpha*. These cases have been categorized as spelling errors, since none of these variations produce a reading which would obviously have been preferred by a copyist, and since the omission and addition of letters has been observed to be a characteristic of this MS.[49]

There are three instances of the addition or omission of words. The article η has been added at 3:5f, as has the conjunction και at 17:32a. These are scribal additions for the sake of a smoother reading.[50] The η has been omitted by error at 17:39.

Readings characteristic of 3004.

Since 3004 is a fragmentary text, its readings have been omitted from the analyses on the preceding pages. In the following paragraphs its text will be examined on the basis of its readings against 149-260. It should be noted that in the present work references to the text of 3004 denote the original

Manuscript Groupings   67

text of that witness. The MS has been corrected on the basis
of de la Cerda's edition.[51] The corrected readings are of no
value in reconstructing the text of the *PssSol*, and have been
ignored except in the collation which appeared in chapter two.[52]

MS 3004 differs from the text of 149-260 eighteen times
in its fifty-seven verses. If the text of this MS had contained
the entire *PssSol*, and had differed from 149-260 to the same
extent throughout, one would have expected to find ninety-three
variants between this MS and 149-260.[53] This fragment may
therefore be described as the least typical member of the 260
group.

The most frequent occurrence of variant readings in 3004
is of spelling changes. Itacism occurs at 17:41f. A final *nu*
has been added to ειοι at 17:27e. An *alpha* is exchanged for an
epsilon at 17:21eg. At 17:6b an *eta* is shortened to an *epsilon*, producing the form ερημωσαν, with a loss of augment. At
17:30f the article το appears as τω, a common scribal error.[54]
Another common error has occurred at 17:22d, where the initial
kappa of καταπατουντων has been read as though it were the
abbreviation for και.[55] At 17:41h the erroneous reading αυτω
has been corrected to αυτοις, probably by the original scribe.[56]

There are several cases of addition or omission in the
text of 3004. Articles have been added to the text in three
places: τον at 17:3d, τα at 17:11f, and αι at 17:19a. Each
of these is an attempt to produce a smoother reading. The
conjunction και is accidentally omitted at 17:12c. Εν απειλη
αυτου φυγειν εθνη απο προσωπου αυτου is missing from 17:25a by
haplography. The word διαψαλμα has been omitted at 17:29 and
at 18:9c. In the last three instances the reading of 3004 is
also shared by MS 471.

Several substitutions have occurred. At 17:32b υπ'
appears in place of επ'. Υπο also appears two words earlier
in all MSS, and 3004 has repeated this word at 17:32b. At
17:33f the singular ελπιδα is read in place of the plural in
all other witnesses. At 18:5 3004 reads αινεσει in place of
αναξει. At 18:10c ημερας is read in place of the less common
term φωστηρας.[57]

68   Psalms of Solomon

Characteristics of the manuscripts of the 260 group.

The most common variant readings among the members of
this group are spelling changes. In addition to spelling
changes, the text of 471-606 has been changed in two instances
under the influence of Septuagintal usage. MS 471 is characterized by the omission of initial letters. A noun form common in
the NT and the LXX appears in 471 in place of a less common
term. Two omissions of διαψαλμα and an omission of a phrase by
haplography have occurred in 471 and 3004. MS 606 includes
spelling variations, some of which have resulted in apparent
changes in wording. This MS has added words on two occasions
in the interest of a smoother text. In proportion to its brief
length, the text of 3004 has departed from the other members
of the group more frequently than any other witness. Its readings include spelling changes and several attempts to improve
the text by the addition of articles or by the substitution of
a more common word for a less familiar term.

The preceding analysis has sustained von Gebhardt's analysis of the relationship between 471 and 606. While many of
their readings are common spelling changes, and so may have
been capable of explanation as simultaneous scribal variants
without genetic significance, it is not likely that the two
agreements at 5:1b and 11:5d are accidental. To account for
these readings a common ancestor must be posited for 471-606
between these witnesses and 149-260. Von Gebhardt represented
the ancestor of 471-606 in the stemma reproduced in the preceding chapter by a lower case *h*.[58]

The extent to which 3004 differs from the other witnesses
of the 260 text group has already been noted. It has been
observed in addition that there are three instances at which 471
agrees with 3004 in omissions against the text of 149-260. With
the exception of the reading at 17:21g, 471 is the only witness
of the 260 group to support the readings of 3004. The majority
of the variants of 3004, however, are not shared by 471. In
addition, there are five readings of 471 in *PsSol* 17:2-18:12
which are not supported by 3004. These include the omission by
471 of the superscription to *PsSol* 18. The agreements which
exist between 3004 and 471 indicate that 3004 is related to the

Manuscript Groupings   69

260 text group by means of the text tradition which also appears
in 471, but the disagreements which exist between the two MSS
prevent 3004 from being considered to be a direct or indirect
copy of 471. That the relationship between 3004 and 471 is by
a common ancestor is indicated by the reading at 17:21g, at
which 3004, 471, and 606 agree in reading ουδας in place of
ουδες, read by 149-260.[59]

A final question remains about the relationship among the
MSS of the 260 group. It has been established that 149 is a
copy of 260, and also that 471, 606, and 3004 are descended
from the text of 149-260 by a common ancestor. The question
remains, however, whether the common ancestor of 471-606-3004
is related to the text of 149-260 through MS 149 or through MS
260. Von Gebhardt's conclusion that the ancestor of 471-606
is based on the relative legibility of the corrections in 149
and 260 at 16:13a. The small *beta* above εν πενια in 260 is
unclear and could be mistaken for an accidental mark, whereas
that in 149 is relatively legible. For this reason, von
Gebhardt concluded that 260 is the MS most likely to have been
misread by a subsequent copyist, and that this witness and not
149 is the exemplar from which the text of 471-606 descended.[60]
The present study has revealed no evidence to require rejecting
this conclusion. A careful approach to historical evidence and
evaluation, however, would suggest that the relative legibility
of two letters may be insufficient evidence for establishing
the historical connections among MSS containing almost three
hundred verses.[61] For the purposes of the present work, the
texts of 149 and 260 will be designated 149-260, and no attempt
will be made to distinguish either as the certain ancestor of
the later witnesses of the 260 group.

The relative reliability of the MSS of the 260 group may
be observed from the foregoing. Exclusive of common spelling
variations, four readings of 149-260 have been observed at
which these MSS preserve a text which is either a probable
original reading or a reading characteristic of older MSS.
These are 1:5c, 5:1b, 11:5d, and 13:6b. By contrast no readings
of 471 or 606 against 149-260 have displayed characteristics of
ancient or probable original readings. There are several readings of MS 3004 which reflect later scribal alterations to the

text. These include 17:3d, 17:11f, 17:19a, 17:22d, 17:25a, and 18:10c. In only one instance, the use of the final *nu* at 17:27e, has 3004 preserved or restored a reading characteristic of an early stage in the textual tradition.

The relationship among the MSS of the 260 group may be represented by the following stemma. In this diagram, q represents the ancestral MS behind 471-606-3004 which was copied directly from 149 or 260. The immediate common ancestor of these MSS is p. The common exemplar between 471 and 3004 is represented by o. The horizontal bracket below 149 and 260 is designed to express the uncertainty over which of these MSS was the exemplar from which q was copied.

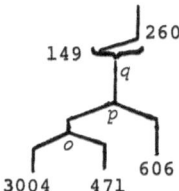

THE 629 GROUP

In the preceding sections of this chapter, readings of the witnesses of each text group have been examined at the points where each MS differs from the majority of its text group. Since the 629 group consists only of two MSS, 629 and 769, the characteristic readings of these MSS will be contrasted to the readings of the majority of the following representatives of the non-629 text groups: MSS 253, 260, and 336.[62] It is to be understood that this procedure is for convenience in presentation only. It should not be inferred that a MS which more closely resembles the witnesses of other text types is thereby the best witness to an earlier stage in the history of its own text group.[63] The study which follows will be limited to the passage where the text of 629 is complete.[64]

Manuscript Groupings   71

Readings where 629 differs from the majority of 253, 260, and 336.

There are fourteen instances at which 629 differs from 769 and the majority of the above witnesses. In three cases, 14:10a, 16:4b, and 16:4d, a final *nu* is omitted by 629. There are four cases of substitution in 629. At 2:36c, τους μετ' αυτου is read by 629 and the 260 group in place of τους οσιους αυτοτυ At 8:1c η ψυχη replaces το ους. At 11:5b βουνοι is read in place of δρυμοι (spelled δριμοι in 769). Βουνοι has probably been copied accidentally from the preceding line. At 14:7b του θεου is read by 629 as αυτου (θεου is omitted by 769). The article η is omitted by 629 and the 253 group at 9:11a. Κυριε has been added at 5:9a. At 11:7f the nonsense reading οιη in the original text of 629 has been corrected to ετι. At 12:1c the original text reads πονηρα, a repetition from the preceding line. This has been corrected to δολια (769 reads δολερα). The article ο has been added before κυριος at 13:4.

Variations between 629 and 769 at which neither is supported by the majority of 253, 260, and 336 will be described below.

Readings where 769 differs from the majority of 253, 260, and 336.

There are thirty-six instances where 769 differs from 629 and the majority of 253, 260, and 336. Over half of these instances are spelling changes. Itacism occurs six times, at 4:17b, 7:8d, 8:9b, 11:5c, 12:3h, and 15:8h. A final *nu* is read seven times: 2:35f, 3:5d, 8:15a, 8:18c, 8:21a, 9:7d, and 13:1b. There are several instances of the addition or omission of a letter. These include the spellings εμπιμπλαται at 4:13b, αγαιασματος at 7:2b, συνενθεντο at 8:10c, ακαρθαρσιας at 8:22c, γνωσσεως at 9:3c, and γλωσης at 12:2f. A *sigma* has been added to υπομονη at 2:36a.[65] Itacism and the addition of an initial *iota* has produced the reading ιχηλεσι in place of χειλεσι at 12:2h. An *alpha iota* and an *epsilon* have been exchanged at 4:1b and 5:12e. There are two variations in the length of the *o*-vowel: 2:31f and 2:32b.

At several readings the wording has been changed by 769. At 8:1d, the words φωνην σαλπιγγος ηκουσης σφαγην και ολεθρον have been added by dittography. The article ου is added by 769 at 12:6e in the interest of a smoother text. θεου has been omitted at 14:7d by confusion of its genitive ending with that of the preceding article του. At 12:6a εστι is read in place of επι. At 4:21a a *kappa* has been read as an abbreviation for και, producing the nonsense reading ου και φοβηθησαν.

The text of 769 has been badly damaged at 13:2ac. The words ρομφαιας διαπορευμενος and και θανατου αμαρτωλων have been intentionally obliterated. The correct words have been rewritten in a modern hand, and are faintly visible in the photographs over the obliterated material. The letters αιασ- διαπυρ, perhaps an earlier attempt at correcting the text, are also visible.[66]

There are several readings where 629 and 769 differ, with neither having the support of a majority of 253, 260, and 336. These are the exchange between *alpha* and *epsilon* at 4:8ab, the spelling of θυσιαστηριον at 8:12bc, the use of the second aorist by 629 and the first aorist by 769 at 13:3e, and the length of the *o*-vowel at 16:5i, where the reading ελογισομαι of the original text of 769 has been corrected to ελογισο με. MS 629 reads ελογισω με.

Characteristics of the manuscripts of the 629 group.

When contrasted to the readings of the majority of 253, 260, and 336, the most frequent readings of 629 are changes in wording. These include the error at 11:5b, the substitutions at 2:36c, 8:1c, 14:7b, and the possible addition of 5:9a. The original reading of 629 has been corrected to that of 769 or to a reading resembling that of 769 at 11:7 and 12:1c. MS 769 is most frequently characterized by spelling variations. The variations in wording which appear in this MS are, with the exception of the addition of the article at 12:6e, attributable to scribal error.[67] The original reading of 769 at 16:5i has been corrected to a reading which differs from that of 629 only in the length of the *o*-vowel.

Manuscript Groupings   73

It is extremely unlikely that either of these MSS is a
copy of the other. Had 629 been the exemplar of 769, it is
unlikely that the latter would not have reproduced the readings
of 629 at 2:36c, 8:1c, and 14:7b. There is nothing in these
readings which would have induced a subsequent copyist to have
emended the text of his exemplar. On the other hand, there are
a large number of readings found in 769 which do not appear in
629. While many of these are common spelling variations and so
could have been changed by a later copyist, the substitution at
2:36c and the aorist form at 13:3e would not likely have been
changed by 629 if they had appeared in its exemplar. It is
unlikely, therefore, that 769 is the exemplar of 629. The
relationship between 629 and 769 is to be found in a common
exemplar standing between these witnesses and the textual tradition of the other MS groups.[68]

There are three instances where the text of one MS has
been corrected to that of the other or to a reading resembling
that of the other. Two of the corrections are not to the reading of the other but to a similar reading from which the other
could have descended by scribal variation. At 12:1 the original
text of 629 erroneously reads πονερα. The reading of 769 is
δολερα. The reading of all other witnesses, to which 629 has
been corrected, is δολια. At 16:5hi the original reading of
769 is ελογισομαι. This has been corrected to ελογισο με. The
reading of 629 is ελογισω με, a reading which differs from the
corrected reading of 769 only by the length of the ο-vowel. In
each of these cases it is unlikely that the corrections have
been made on the basis of the other MS. The corrections are
more likely to have reproduced the text of the common exemplar
behind 629 and 769. At 12:1c, the exemplar reads δολια along
with all other MSS, and was misread by the copyists of 629 and
769. We may infer that the writing of the exemplar at this
point was unclear. At 16:5hi the original reading of 769,
ελογισομαι, has been corrected to ελογισο με by an *epsilon* which
has been written above the final *alpha iota*. The spelling
ελογισο is a misspelling of the aorist indicative ελογισω,
which appears in 629. Rather than assuming that the exemplar
spelled incorrectly and was corrected by the copyist of 629,
it is more likely that the scribe of 769 corrected ελογισομαι

to ελογισο με by writing the *epsilon* above the error, but neglected to correct the *omicron* to the *omega* which appeared in the exemplar and which was preserved by 629.

There are ten instances where 629 and 769 differ with regard to the final *nu*. The final *nu* is characteristically read by 769 and omitted by 629. Since the omission of the final *nu* is normally a characteristic of later MSS, it is likely that the *nu* was read by the exemplar and omitted by 629. This is in keeping with the observed tendency of 629 to introduce emendations to the text. MS 769, on the other hand, has introduced no substantive alterations except the addition of one article, and, although a later MS, has preserved the final *nu* of the exemplar.

The exemplar of 629-769 may be described as having contained the text which 769 has preserved with numerous spelling changes. MS 629 has avoided many of these spelling errors, but has introduced several changes in wording. Although 629 is an earlier MS, it is a less reliable witness than 769 to the original text of its group.

The relationship between 629 and 769 may be depicted by the following stemma:

In this representation, *n* denotes the common exemplar behind the texts of 629 and 769.

The characteristic readings of the MS groups will be examined in the following chapter.

CHAPTER FIVE

TEXTUAL CHARACTERISTICS OF THE TEXT TYPES

Four distinct text types or groupings of the MSS of the *PssSol* were identified in chapter three. These are the 253 group, the 260 group, the singular MS 336, and the 629 group. Chapter four examined readings of the component witnesses of the 253, 260, and 629 groups in order to determine the textual characteristics of the MSS and to ascertain the relationships among the witnesses of each text group.[1] The present chapter will use a procedure similar to that employed in chapter four to identify the textual characteristics of each MS group. The evidence obtained in this chapter will be used in the following chapter to establish the relationship among the groups and the history of their transmission.

The basis of the study in the present chapter will be the representative readings of each text type. For the 253 group, these will be readings read by MS 253 and at least one other group member. These readings may be taken to be characteristic of the entire 253 group and not peculiarities of MS 253 or of the common ancestor of 655-659.[2] The 260 group will be represented by the readings of MS 260, the ancestral MS of that group. The text type of MS 336 will be represented by that MS. Since there are no other extant witnesses of this text type, there are no means for distinguishing readings characteristic of the 336 textual tradition from readings which have resulted in scribal variations in the transmission of that tradition or in the copying of MS 336 itself.[3] The 629 group will be represented by those readings which are supported by both 629 and 769, and which therefore preserve the original text of that group.

This chapter will discuss the representative readings of each text type as they appear as readings found in only one text group, as readings shared by two groups, and as readings of three groups against a fourth. For convenience in organizing the material, the section immediately to follow will discuss readings found only in one group in contrast to the readings of the remaining groups. The next section will discuss readings shared by two groups. Readings shared by three groups against a fourth will appear in the former section as the contrasting background against which the readings of single groups will be displayed.

READINGS OF SINGLE GROUPS

The present section will examine the representative readings which are supported only by the witnesses of one text group.

Readings of the 253 Group.

There are 221 readings at which 253 and either 655 or 659 differ from the representatives of the other text groups. Sixty-five of these variations are spelling changes. Itacism occurs twenty-six times. Examples are the spelling of the dative ισχυι as ισχυει by 253-655-659 at 2:29e, 17:36c, and 17:38b. Among the instances of itacism in this group are readings where apparent grammatical alterations have been produced. At 2:21c the subjunctive verb απερριφη is found in the 253 group as the indicative απερριφει. The 253 group reads the indicative επιτιμησεις in place of the subjunctive επιτιμησης at 2:23d.[4] There are twenty-one readings where the 253 group differs from the non-253 witnesses in preserving the archaic final νu.[5] There are four instances of variation in the length of the o-vowel. At 2:34 the *omicron* of μεσον is lengthened to an *omega* by 253-655-659. An *omega* is shortened to an *omicron* at 3:4a, 13:9b, and 15:10a.[6] There are five readings at which apparent changes in wording have resulted from spelling variations. At 4:8f μονον is read in place of νομον. At 4:8g δουλου appears in place of δολου. Ευχρηστος is read at 5:2c in place of συ χρηστος. At 5:11bc 253 and 655-659 read στρεφεις and στεφεις, respectively, in place of τρεφεις.[7] At 8:31 the 253 group reads η ελπις ημων for ηλπισαμεν, read by all other witnesses. That the common ancestor between the 253 group and the other witnesses is an uncial MS is demonstrated by three of

Text-type Characteristics   77

these variations: 4:8f MONON for NOMON, 5:2a ΕΥΧΡΗCTOC for
CΥΧΡΗCTOC, and 8:31 ΗΕΛΠΙCΗΜΩΝ for ΕΛΠΙCΑΜΕΝ.[8]
Thirty of the variations involving the 253 group are verb
changes. The most frequent of these are the rejection of the
strong endings of the imperfect and second aorist in favor of
the sigmatic -οσαν endings of the first aorist.[9] These changes
have occurred eighteen times. In eight of these instances the
ending occurs with the unmodified stem of the imperfect and
first aorist.[10] Examples are the readings at 2:2a and 8:12a,
where the 253 group reads κατεπατουσαν and πατουσαν while the
other witnesses read κατεπατουν and πατουν.[11] In ten cases the
ending occurs with the modified or strong stem of the second
aorist. Three of these variations are between ειπα, read by
the 253 group, and ειπον, read by the other groups.[12] Two
instances involve the verb φευγω: the 253 group reads εφυγοσαν
at 11:4b and 17:16a, while the non-253 groups read εφυγον. The
253 group has preserved readings characteristic of early
Hellenistic usage in each of these cases.[13]

There are three instances of change in the number of a
verb. At 4:16c the optative singular αποπεσοι is read as
αποπεσοιεν by the 253 group. Καταδιωξεται at 15:8a appears in
253-655-659 as the plural καταδιωξονται. Καταλημψεται is read
as καταλημψονται at 15:8e. In addition, there are four apparent changes in the number of a verb which are in reality readings produced by the exchange of an *epsilon* for an *alpha*. In each of these instances, 4:20c, 4:20e, 4:21e, and 8:22d, plural verbs are required by the context.

There are eighteen changes in nouns or adjectives in the
253 text group. The most frequent of these are changes from
second declension masculine to third declension neuter forms,
occurring ten times. Eight of these instances involve the noun
ελεος. The third declension genitive ελεους is read by the
253 group at 2:8c, 8:28b, 14:9c, 17:3e, 18:3a, and 18:9a. At
5:12c the third declension dative ελεει is read in place of
the second declension ελεω of the non-253 text groups. The
neuter third declension is preferred in the LXX and the NT.
Attic style prefers the masculine second declension.[14] On two
occasions, 2:24a and 4:3e, the dative singular of ζηλος is
read by the 253 group as the third declension ζηλει in place

of the second declension ζηλω. Both second and third declension forms are found in the NT. Second declension masculine forms are preferred in the LXX and are the rule in Attic Greek.[15]

Changes in the number of a noun or adjective occur six times in the 253 group. Examples are 2:22e, where the singular χειρα is read as the plural χειρας by 253-655-659, and 4:10a, where the singular αδικου is read as αδικων.[16]

There are two instances of change in the gender of the adjective πας. At 3:8d and 8:20b this adjective, followed in each case by a masculine singular accusative substantive, appears in the witnesses of the other text groups as the masculine singular accusative παντα. In the 253 group, however, the adjective is the neuter παν. The use of παν with a masculine accusative substantive is an extremely unusual occurrence, and may be restricted to the Greek of the LXX where, however, it appears less than thirty times.[17]

There are eighteen instances of additions in the 253 group. In the majority of these cases, articles or conjunctions have been added in an effort to produce a smoother reading. Examples include the addition of και at 2:25a, του at 2:32a, η at 3:12a, and τον at 17:30c.[18] Μη is added following ου at 3:11a. The use of ου μη with the future indicative, as in this instance, is common in the Greek of the LXX and the NT.[19] While it is possible that 253 has added μη in accordance with this usage, it is also possible that μη was part of the original text of the *PssSol*, and was accidentally omitted from the uncial form OUMHMNHCΘHCETAI by confusion with the similar letters *mu nu* which follow.[20]

There are thirty-three cases of omissions. The most frequent omissions are of articles. This has occurred twelve times.[21] A και has been omitted at 4:3e and 4:15c. There are two instances of omissions by haplography. At 4:16h-4:17a the words εν ατιμια κενος χερσιν αυτου εισελθοι εις τον οικον αυτου have been omitted. At 12:5b the words ψυχην ησουχιον μισουσαν αδικους και κατευθυναι κυριος are missing. There are two instances of omissions caused by the confusion of a word with the similar ending of the preceding word. At 2:6b the article αι is missing following και. At 14:2d the relative pronoun ω is

Text-type Characteristics 79

absent following νομω.²² Seven omissions are of an article attached to a noun with a following genitive personal pronoun²³ or of a genitive personal pronoun attached to a noun with a preceding article.²⁴ Although such omissions are not a rule throughout the 253 group readings, these instances preserve an early stage of the text, since Greek translated from semitic sources does not normally combine the use of articles with following genitive personal pronouns.²⁵

There are twelve transpositions. Examples are the reading βεβηλε καθησαι in place of καθησαι βεβηλε and καθησε βεβηλε at 4:1a and εισιν αυτων in place of αυτων εισι and αυτων εισιν at 17:27de.²⁶

There are fifteen instances of substitutions in 253-655-659. At 2:13c and 9:5b the reflexive pronouns εαυτας and εαυτω appear as αυτας and αυτω, respectively. Reflexive pronouns without the initial *epsilon* had become unusual by the second century B.C.E., and are rare in the LXX and NT.²⁷ At 3:4c the 253 group reads εναντι for εναντιον, the more familiar term in the NT. At 14:8c ταμεια is read in place of ταμιεια. The contracted form supplanted ταμιεια by the first centuries C.E., and is the usual NT form.²⁸ In each of these instances, the 253 group has preserved ancient or probable original readings. The substitution of επι for μετα at 18:1a is a scribal error. Επι was repeated from the previous line in an error which was facilitated by the identical pronoun σου which precedes each instance.²⁹

Readings of the 260 Group.

There are sixty-two instances where MS 260 reads differently from the representatives of the other text types. Nineteen of these are spelling variants. There are three readings at which an *alpha* and an *epsilon* have been exchanged: 2:11a, 2:22h, and 3:10a. Itacism occurs at 2:23b, where μηνησεως is read in place of μηνισεως, and 5:2b, where ει appears for η. At 2:5b a scribe has substituted the more common εξουθενηθη for the less familiar εξουθενωθη.³⁰ At 16:12a 260 reads στηριξον in place of στηρισον as the aorist imperative. The spelling of the non-260 readings is the rule in the LXX.[31] The usage of the NT varies.[32]

There are six apparent variations in wording which have resulted from spelling errors. At 5:13a 260 reads φιλω in place of φειδω. With the exception of the itacism, the difference between these words is the result of confusion between an uncial *lambda* and *delta*: the ancestor of the 260 group has read ΦΙΛΩ for ΦΕΙΔΩ. At 12:2gh 260 reads αλω for λαω. the uncial form of these are the almost identical ΑΛΩ and ΛΑΩ. The difference between the readings of the 260 group and the other text types at 12:2j is also derived from an uncial stage in the transmission of the text: for the reading of the other groups, ΚΑΛΛΟΝΗΝ, the 260 group has read ΚΑΛΑΜΗΝ. The non-260 witnesses read καινον at 15:3a. The 260 text has incorrectly taken the initial *kappa* to be the abbreviation for και, and has produced the reading και αινον.[33] The reading of 260 at 17:6d is the result of an *alpha* having been erroneously added to the uncial text, producing the reading ΑΛΑΛΑΓΜΑΤΟΣ. A confusion between an *omicron* and an *epsilon* has produced the reading ανεμος for ανομος at 17:11c.[34]

There are five instances of change in case in the 260 group. At 5:4 the dative pronoun σοι appears in place of the genitive σου. At 6:4c and 6:4g the 260 group reads the accusative το ονομα for the dative τω ονοματι. The dative αυτοις appears in place of the accusative αυτους at 8:14b. At 17:23f 260 reads αμαρτωλους in place of αμαρτωλου, read by the 253 and 629 groups, and αμαρτωλων, read by 336. The preceding verb εξωσαι is the aorist imperative of εξωθεω, which occurs twenty-six times in the LXX and twice in the NT. Moulton and Milligan identify three occurrences of εξωθεω in the papyri.[35] The accusative case is used for the object of the verb throughout. The reading of the 260 text group has placed the object in the accusative, and so has conformed the text to the usage of the LXX.[36]

There are two changes in number in the 260 group. At 8:17d the pronoun αυτου is read as the plural αυτων. At 17:43g the participle ηγιασμενου appears as the plural ηγιασμενων.

There are ten instances of additions in the 260 group. Three of the cases involve the preposition εν: 4:15b, 11:1c, and 11:8. An article has been added in three places: 5:11a, 14:5c, and 15:12a. The added relative pronoun α at 17:44d is induced by the change in the following verb from an infinitive to an indicative. Ανθρωπος has been added at 5:3d. The pronoun συ appears following ευλογημενος at 8:34b. This is an original reading which has been omitted from the other groups by confusion in the uncial form of συ in και συ ευλογημενος: ΚΑΙCΥΕΥΛΟΓΗΜΕΝΟC.[37]

There are five omissions in 260. Οσιω at 4:1c has been omitted by haplography. The omission of εως at 2:5d and γαρ at 10:4c may have been induced by the similarly-appearing initial letters of the following words εις and μαρτυρια.[38] Other omissions are of οικον at 4:11a and ως αδης at 4:13d.

Substitutions have occurred thirteen times in the 260 group. On three occasions the preposition εν appears in place of other prepositions or the article η: 4:9b, 8:4, and 14:7.[39] Επι appears for η at 9:2b. At 2:27a διεφθαρμενον is read for διαφερομενον. At 4:15d the 260 group has incorrectly copied οδυναις from the preceding line. At 9:5 αδικα is read as an adjectival substantive in place of the noun αδικιαν. Αυτους appears at 17:9d in place of the less usual construction αυτων ενα, perhaps under the influence of Ps 104:14. Εν φοβω is read at 18:8b in place of ενωπιον. Other instances are 4:10b, 5:16a, 12:2a, 12:2d, and 18:4e.

There are two instances of transposition in the 260 group. The transposition involving εν πευια παιδειαν at 16:13b has been discussed in the preceding chapter. The words αποδουναι αμαρτωλοις εις τον αιωνα χρονον, which appear in the 260 group at 15:12d, the end of the verse, are found spelled απολουνται αμαρτωλοι in varying word order at the end of the following verse in the non-260 group witnesses. The spelling variation is an error of the 260 group, in which the uncial form ΑΠΟΛΟΥΝΤΑΙ has been read as ΑΠΟΔΟΥΝΑΙ.[40] The reading of 336 is closest to that of the 260 group, preserving the same word order and differing only in spelling. There are several reasons for preferring the word order of the 260 group. At 16:13b, the only other instance of transposition in the 260 group, MS 260 has indicated the correct word order. There is no such indication in this MS at 15:12-13. In addition, it is more persuasive to assume that a line has been omitted by the non-260 groups and added a verse later than to suppose that a line, properly located in the non-260 MSS at the end of verse 13, has been transposed forward by the copyist of the 260 group.[41]

Readings of 336.

There are 106 readings where 336 differs from the representative witnesses of the non-336 text types. Thirty-two of these are spelling variations. There are ten variations in the length of the *o*-vowel. In five instances an *omicron* is read as an *omega* by 336: 12:2i, 12:4d, 16:5f, 16:9b, and 16:11b. The variation at 16:9f was induced by the preceding εν: the scribe wrote an *omega* in the first syllable of τοπω in anticipation of the dative article τω. An *omega* in the non-336 witnesses is read as an *omicron* in five cases: 2:19b, 8:17a, 15:9b, 15:9c, and 16:1a. The shortened vowel at 2:19b and 8:17a has resulted in the loss of the augment from ωνειδισαν and ωμαλισαν. There are three instances of itacism: 4:22b, 12:3b, and 18:4f.[42] A letter has been added in three instances. At 14:4d and 15:2f a *lambda* and a *sigma* have been doubled, respectively, producing the readings εκτιλλησονται and εξομολογησασσθαι. A *kappa* has been added to the article at 15:11c, resulting in the reading και. Letters have been omitted in eight instances. Six of these are the omission of initial letters at the beginnings of lines: 3:12e, 11:7d, 13:8, 13:10a, 13:11a, and 13:11b. At 9:6i παντων has been read in place of απαντων. The non-336 reading is less well attested in the LXX: απας is not normally found following a vowel.[43] The *eta* has been omitted from πληθυναι at 10:1e. There are three variations involving an exchange between an *alpha* and an *epsilon*: 2:36d, 17:15b, and 17:18c. Ηρημωσαν is spelled with an initial *epsilon* at 17:6b and 17:11b, with a resulting loss of augment. The apparent change at 2:4b to an aorist indicative has resulted from the substitution of an uncial *epsilon* for an *omicron*, a common error.[44] A similar substitution of an *upsilon* for an *epsilon* has produced the reading υπεθεντο at 17:5b.

Text-type Characteristics   83

There are several grammatical changes in the readings of 336. There are nine instances of change in case. These include the erroneous use of the dative σου at 5:8b and 9:8b and the use of ημων for ημιν, reproducing the form of the previous pronoun at 17:5a. At 17:18e the genitive της γης follows επι in place of την γην.[45] Other changes in case have occurred at 12:3i, 12:6b, 14:2c, 15:3e, and 15:7c. In none of these instances has the reading of 336 represented an improvement of the text or a probable original reading. There are six changes in the number of a noun or pronoun. Of these four are changes of the personal pronoun from the genitive singular αυτων to the singular αυτου: 2:8d, 4:9a, 11:1d, and 17:20a. At 17:12a the genitive singular has been replaced by the genitive plural. In each of these instances except that of 4:9a, the pronoun has been made to agree in number with the substantive to which it is attached rather than with its antecedent. At 8:34a the dative singular στοματι appears as the plural στομασιν, apparently for agreement in number with the following genitive plural pronoun αυτων. There is one instance of a change from a noun to a verb: at 2:19d the aorist infinitive καταπατησαι appears in place of the prepositional phrase εν καταπατησει.

The most frequent of the variations involving verbs are changes in tense. At 15:2c the present ισχυει is read by 336 as the future ισχυσει. The opposite occurs at 17:3b, where ελπιζομεν is read in place of ελπιουμεν. At 17:10b 336 reads the aorist εποιησεν in place of the present ποιει. At 10:7b the aorist subjunctive δοξασωσι appears in place of the future indicative δοξασουσι, read by the non-336 witnesses.[46] The substitution of the aorist subjunctive for the future indicative, which initially resulted from the phonetic similarity between the two forms, is attested in the NT and becomes the rule in later Greek usage.[47] The future indicative αφησει appears at 17:40e as the aorist infinitive αφησαι, probably by conformity to the following aorist infinitive ασθενησαι.[48] A present subjunctive is read as present indicative by 336 in two instances: 3:11c and 5:6a. In each of these instances the use of the subjunctive is preferred.[49] There are two grammatical variations involving the infinitive. At 2:24d an infinitive in

the non-336 witnesses is read as a participle. At 17:24 an
imperative appears in place of an infinitive.
There are eighteen additions in 336 of material which is
not found in the non-336 witnesses. There are three additions
by dittography. At 2:35d the words αποδουναι αμαρτωλοις εις
τον αιωνα κατα τα εργα αυτων are repeated from the preceding
line. In both instances the words are preceded by αμαρτωλου.
At 10:5e εις τον αιωνα follows κυριου. The same words follow
the genitive singular personal pronoun in the preceding line in
all witnesses. At 17:1c the composite phrase εις τον αιωνα ο
θεος ημων και is added by 336. There are six additions of
articles: 3:9a, 3:9b, 4:8e, 4:13c, 13:3h, and 15:1c. Verbs
have been added in two cases: ει at 15:1e and γενεσθαι at
16:1k. Other readings not found in the non-336 witnesses are
ου at 2:26b, αυτων at 8:33b, εν at 10:5c, εις σοτηριαν at
16:3d, and και at 17:5g.

There are fifteen omissions in 336. Eleven of these are
the absence of single words. In five cases, articles have been
omitted: 4:1e, 8:15e, 9:2e, 11:2a, and 17:13e. In the last
three cases the articles are attached to nouns with following
genitive personal pronouns. The omission of these articles is
characteristic of Greek which has been translated from semitic
sources.[50] MS 336 has preserved probable original readings
by these omissions. Nouns are omitted in three instances:
2:22c, 8:24b, and 17:37d. In the last two instances the omission was produced by confusion with the endings of the preceding
words. The preposition εις is absent at 11:2b. The dative
personal pronoun σοι is omitted at 15:2c. At 17:43h the conjunction ως is omitted.

There are five larger portions of text which are not
found in MS 336. The largest is the lacuna from the end of
5:14 to the beginning of 8:12. Beginning at 16:4a, 336 omits
the following: ενυξεν με εως κεντρον ιππου επι την γρηγορησιν
αυτου, ο σωτηρ και αντιληπτωρ μου εν παντι καιρω εσωσεν με.
εξομολογησομαι σοι, ο θεος, οτι αντελαβου μου εις σωτηριαν.
The words απο αμαρτιας πονηρας και απο πασης γυναικος πονηρας
σκανδαλιζουσης αφρονα και are omitted beginning at 16:7a. At
17:21d, the following is omitted: εις τον καιρον, ον ειλου σου,
ο θεος, του βασιλευσαι επι Ισραηλ παιδα σου. The following is

Text-type Characteristics 85

absent from 336 at 17:32e: οτι παντες αγιοι, και βασιλευς αυτων χριστος κυριου. It is not possible to show that these are either omissions by 336 or additions by the other MSS. There are no resemblances between the beginnings and ends of these passages and the surrounding materials such as would have induced haplography,[51] nor are they sufficiently attractive to have been added to the text by the copyists of the other text groups.[52] There are no compelling affinities with passages of the LXX or of the NT.[53]

There are several cases of substitution in 336. In three instances Ιερουσαλημ is read in place of Ισραηλ: 9:1c, 17:42, and 17:44c. The words θεος and κυριος have been exchanged three times. At 3:2b 336 reads κυριω in place of θεω. The opposite has occurred at 16:3c and 17:10a, where θεος is read for κυριος. Two substitutions have been induced by the ease by which similar uncial letters can be added or omitted: ATIMIAMIA for ATIMIA or AITIAMIA at 2:25e, and ΨΑΛΑΙ for ΨΑΛΛΕ ΚΑΙ at 3:2a. The reading εγερσις at 4:15e is the substitution by the scribe of a more familiar word for a less common term: the 336 reading appears four times in the LXX and the NT,[54] whereas the non-336 reading, εξεγερσις, is not attested elsewhere. The reading υπνωσα for ωλισθησα at 16:1e is likewise an attempt to improve upon a difficult reading. In two instances 336 preserves an uncommon and more likely original reading. At 9:6a 336 reads χρησιμευσει for χρηστευση. The verb in 336 appears elsewhere in the LXX only at Wis 4:3 and Sir 13:4, and in these passages the term is used to denote grasping by the ungodly and the rich. The word κατωτατου, read by 336 for κατω at 15:10c, follows εως αδου in the LXX only at Tobit 4:19 and 13:2 in Codex Sinaiticus. The substitution of σπερμα for πτωμα at 3:10d probably represents the last of two alterations to the text. The first was the substitution of σωμα as a synonym for πτωμα during an uncial stage of the text. The latter was considered to be an indelicate or undignified term.[55] Apparently σωμα had been abbreviated $\overline{CMA}$. The latter was read by the copyist as the abbreviation for σπερμα.[56] Other substitutions have occurred at 2:22b, 5:3c, 17:5b, and 17:23h.

Readings of the 629 Group.

There are only twenty readings at which 629 and 769 agree against the representative witnesses of the other text groups. Of these, just four are unambiguous spelling variations. The reading at 3:8e, at which the 629 group reads θειον for οσιον, was induced by the similarity between the uncial forms ΘΕΙΟΝ and ΟCΙΟΝ. An itacism has occurred at 9:6b. The reading at 8:9d, θυτρος for θυγατρος, was induced by the similarity of an uncial *tau* to a *gamma*, allowing the syllable to have been omitted. At 15:3g 629-769 read απαρχη for απαρχην, read by the 253 and 260 groups.[57] Although this reading has apparently produced a change to a nominative or dative singular, it is in this instance an erroneous omission of a final *nu*, since the accusative case is demanded by the context.

There are two changes in case. The verb at 4:2e, which appears as a participle in the 260 group and as an aorist infinitive in 253 and 336, is read by the 629 group as the present or future indicative κατακρινει. The aorist subjunctive επακουση at 7:7b is read by 629-769 as the future indicative επακουσεις. There is one change in gender. At 8:3d the masculine or neuter form αυτον appears in 629-769 as the feminine αυτην.[58]

There are three instances of additions. At 8:2c the words ως ανεμου πολλου have been added by dittography from the preceding line. At 14:8b and 15:13d the articles τα and οι have been added.[59] There are seven omissions. At 5:3b the words ου γαρ ληψεται σκυλα παρα ανδρος δυνατου have been omitted by haplography, as has the passage 13:6d-13:7a. Other omissions have occurred at 7:7a, 8:33a, 10:2d, 15:4b, and 16:1h.

There are two transpositions. At 4:20d the words πολλους ανθρωπων are transposed with a change in case, and appear in the 629 group as ανθρωπων πολλων.. This transposition was induced by the similar endings of πολλους and the preceding word οικους, as a result of which πολλους was omitted and reinserted following ανθρωπων, but with a genitive plural ending. At 11:7d Ισραηλ has been moved to the end of the verse. This may have occurred due to the similar pronunciation of its first syllable to that of the following word εις.

Text-type Characteristics 87

There are two instances of substitution in the 629 group, both of which involve the word κυριου. Κυριου is replaced by αυτου at 2:33b, and by θεου at 15:8i.

READINGS OF GROUPS IN COMBINATION

In the previous section of this chapter an examination was made of readings supported by the representative witnesses of single groups against the readings of the other text groups. Readings supported by combinations of two text groups will be examined in the present section.[60]

Readings of the 253 and 260 Groups against 336 and the 629 Group.

There are twelve readings shared by the 253 and 260 groups against the readings of the other text types. Of these, seven represent spelling variants. There are two variations in the use of the final *nu*. The final *nu* is read by the 253 group and 149-260 at 1:5cd, and is omitted by these witnesses at 2:9a. Itacism in 336 and 769 at 2:21b has produced the erroneous reading μητραν.[61] The reading of a present for an aorist infinitive by the 253 and 260 groups at 17:4d was caused by itacism. There are two instances of the omission of letters. At 2:14 the *gamma* in σπλαγχνα is omitted in 336 and 769.[62] The omission of this letter may represent a phonetic rather than a spelling variation.[63] At 18:9b the final *alpha* is omitted from διαψαλμα by the 253 and 260 groups. The apparent change between the present infinitive and imperative forms of ερχομαι at 17:31a is the result of the variation between *alpha* *iota* and *epsilon*, a common scribal change.[64]

There are two instances of change in case. At 2:23g the dative pronoun αυτοις is read by 336 and 769 as the accusative αυτους.[65] The preceding verb επιτιμησης occurs twelve times in the LXX, and takes a dative object throughout.[66] In later Greek, however, datives came to be replaced by accusatives. This became the rule by the tenth century.[67] The reading of 336 and 769 therefore probably represents a later alteration to the text. At 8:33c the 253 and 260 groups read the vocative κυριε in place of the nominative of the other groups. This noun is used eighteen times in the *Psalms* to address the deity.[68] In virtually all of these instances the vocative is used. The only exception, in addition to the instance at 8:33c, is 2:22c, where the word is omitted by 336. Κυριε is probably the original reading. The use of the nominative is attested in the LXX and the NT;[69] 336 and the 629 group has followed that latter usage.

There are two substitutions. At 10:8cd the 253 and 260 groups read εις σωφροσυνην for εις ευφροσυνην, the reading of 336 and the 629 group.[70] The latter is most likely to be correct: ευφροσυνην better fits the surrounding context, and appears twice in the preceding three verses. The reading of the 253 and 260 groups is an unusual term, occurring only nine times in the LXX.[71] The substitution is to be explained by the similarity of the uncial forms: EICEUΦPOCUNHN has been replaced by EICCΩΦPOCUNHN. At 15:7e 336 and the 629 group read θειων for οσιων. This variation is identical to that of the 629 group at 3:8e, a discussion of which has appeared on a previous page.[72]

Readings of the 253 Group and 336 against the 260 and 629 Groups.

There are twelve readings where the 253 group and 336 agree against the representatives of the other text types. Five of these are spelling variations. Itacism occurs three times. At 2:36e shares with the 253 group the spelling ισχυει for ισχυι. This spelling is read by the 253 group alone at 2:29b, 17:36c, and 17:38b. Itacism has also occurred at 4:9c and at 5:8a. An exchange of an *alpha iota* for an *epsilon* has produced the reading αισχατου at 8:15c.[73] A variation in the length of the *o*-vowel has produced ανοφελους at 16:8d.

The sigmatic -σαν ending has replaced -εν for the third person plural aorist optative in the 253 group and 336 at 4:8a. This form is characteristic of Koine Greek, and is attested in the LXX. The reading of the 260 and 629 groups may be an Atticizing correction by a copyist.[74] A change in number has occurred at 5:10h, where the 260 and 629 groups read the plural προσωπα for προσωπον.

Text-type Characteristics   89

There are two cases of addition and omission. At 3:12b
the article η, read by the 253 group and 336, is omitted by the
other witnesses, probably by assimilation to the final vowel of
the preceding word αυτη. At 9:4a the preposition εν is omitted
by the 253 group and 336.
There are three substitutions in the 253 group and 336.
At 3:2c these witnesses read αγαθης in place of ολης, read by
the MSS of the other text groups. The latter reading is a
scribal assimilation to the usage of the LXX Psalms, in which
the words εν ολη καρδια occur nine times.[75] The use of αγαθη
with καρδια, as in the reading preserved by the 253 group and
336, is without parallel in the LXX Psalter. At 17:35a the 253
group and 336 read καταξει for παταξει. At 17:41b 253 and 336,
together with the corrected text of 769, read ισοτητι for
οσιοτητι. The four words in which this variation is found are
omitted by 655 and 659. The reading of 253 and 336 is an uncommon word, found only twice in the LXX.[76] The 260 and 629
group reading is a scribal substitution, induced by the ease
by which the initial letters could be transposed to produce the
more familiar οσιοτητι.

Readings of the 253 and 629 Groups against the 260 Group and 336.
There are thirteen readings at which the 253 and 629
groups agree against the readings of the other text groups.
Seven of these readings are spelling variations. Itacism has
occurred twice, at 1:3c, where, in addition, the doubling of
the *lambda* has produced the reading πολλην for πολυν, and 4:17b,
there ελλειπης is read for ελλιπης. The archaic final *nu* is
read by the 253 and 629 groups at 2:8a, 4:10c, and 17:9c. At
3:1a the reading και αινον is found in the 253 and 629 groups
in place of καινον. This is the same variation as that found
in the 260 group at 15:3a, discussed above. The initial *kappa*
of καινον has been read as an abbreviation for και.[77] The
original text of 3:1a was an allusion to Psalm 39:4: εις το
στομα μου ασμα καινον τω θεω ημων.[78] A variation in the length
of the *o*-vowel has occurred at 6:3de, where the 253 and 629
groups read σαλον for σαλων.

There are four instances of addition and omission among these witnesses. At 2:31a the article ο is read by the 253 and 629 groups. At 4:8d οι is read by the 260 group and 336. The latter witnesses read a second και at 5:13. A η precedes κληρονομια in the 260 group and 336 at 14:5b. This article, which is also read by 655-659, has been added to create a parallel structure to that of η μερις, which, with κληρονομια, forms a compound object to the clause. A substitution occurs at 4:21c, where πασι is read by the 260 group and 336 in place of απασι, read by the 253 and 629 groups. This variation is the same as that which occurred in 336 at 9:6i. In the present instance the usage of the 260 group and 336 follows that of the LXX.[79] A transposition occurs at 13:6df, at which ουδεν follows τουτων in the 260 group and 336. Ουδεν and the entire following verse are omitted by the 629 group. The transposition was probably induced by the similarity of the first syllable of ουδεν to the last syllable of the preceding word δικαιου. Ουδεν was therefore accidentally omitted and replaced later in the text.

CHARACTERISTICS OF THE TEXT TYPES

It will be useful at this point to review the working definition of a textual characteristic which was presented in the previous chapter. A textual characteristic, in the case of a MS or group which has fewer than one hundred variations from the other witnesses with which comparison is being made, is a category of readings of which two examples exist in that MS or group. For a MS or group which has one hundred or more variations, the number of examples must equal two percent of the total number of variants. This definition will be used as a basis for describing the textual characteristics of the *PsSol* text types. The descriptions of the textual characteristics which follow will be used in chapter six to establish the relationship among the MS groups.

Text-type Characteristics

Characteristics of the 253 Group.

There are 221 readings at which the 253 group differs from the other text groups. Sixty-five of these variations are spelling changes. These include itacisms, the use of the variable final *nu* by the 253 group, variations in the length of the *o*-vowel, exchanges between an *alpha* and an *epsilon*, and variations arising from similarities between uncial forms. Verb changes comprise thirty of the variations. The most frequent verb changes involve the use of sigmatic aorist endings by the 253 group. Eighteen of the readings are changes in nouns or adjectives, of which the majority are the use of neuter third declension forms by the 253 group. Eighteen of the variants involve the presence in the 253 group of material not found in the other text groups. The majority of these are the addition of articles and conjunctions by the 253 group. Thirty-three variations involve the omission by the 253 group of material read by the other text groups. The most frequent is the absence of articles found in the non-253 witnesses. Seven of the total number of variations involve readings where the other text types combine the use of an article with a following genitive personal pronoun. In these latter instances, the 253 group readings are characteristic of Greek translated from semitic sources, and so are probable original readings. Transpostions and substitutions are also found among the readings of the 253 group.

There are sixteen instances where the 253 group shares with the 260 group readings against the other text types. Seven of these are spelling variations, including itacism and the omission of letters by these groups. There are two instances of change in case, at which the 253 and 260 groups preserve probable original readings. There are two substitutions, both involving the confusion of similar uncial forms. The 253 group shares twelve readings with 336. Five of these are spelling variants, of which itacism is the most common. There are three substitutions, at each of which the 253 group and 336 preserve probable original readings. There are thirteen readings shared by the 253 and 629 groups. Of these, seven are spelling variations, including itacism and the presence of the final *nu*. There are three instances at which words found in the other text groups are omitted from the 253 and 629 groups.

The textual characteristics of the 253 group as they have been observed in the singular readings of that group and in combination with other groups may be summarized in graphic form by the following:

Characteristic:[80]	253 alone	Combined with: 260	336	629
Verb changes	X			
Transportation	X			
Omissions and additions	X			X
Substitutions	X	X	X	
Case changes	X			
Spelling Changes	X	X	X	X

There are fifty instances at which singular readings of the 253 group have been identified as probable original readings or as readings characteristic of an earlier stage in the textual tradition. These include twenty-one instances of the preservation of the archaic final *nu*, eighteen instances of the use of strong aorist endings, seven cases at which the use of articles together with following genitive personal pronouns has occurred in the non-253 witnesses, and the substitutions at 2:13c, 3:4c, 9:5b, and 14:8c.

Characteristics of the 260 Group.

There are sixty-three cases at which the representative MS of the 260 group, MS 260, reads differently from the other text types. Nineteen of these are spelling variants, including the exchange between *alpha* and *epsilon*, itacism, and spelling derived from uncial forms. There are five changes in case and two changes in number. In six cases the preposition εν or an article, not found in the non-260 witnesses, are read by 260. There are five omissions of material which is found in other groups. There are thirteen instances of substitutions, many of which represent scribal variations in the 260 text tradition. There are two transpositions.

There are readings shared by 260 and the 253 group. These have been characterized in the preceding section. There are thirteen readings shared by the 260 group and 336. These readings are the converse of the readings shared by the 253 and 629 groups, described on the previous page. These include itacism and other spelling variations, including the absence in the 260 group and 336 of the final *nu*. In three cases material that is absent from the other text groups is read by the 260 group and 336. There are twelve shared readings between the 260 and 629 groups. These include itacism and other spelling variations and three substitutions.

The following summarizes the textual characteristics of the 260 group:

Characteristic:	260 alone	Combined with: 253	336	629
Verb changes				
Transpositions		X		
Omissions and additions	X		X	
Substitutions	X	X		X
Case changes	X	X		
Spelling changes	X	X	X	X

There are two probable original readings preserved only by the 260 group: the retention of συ at 8:34b and the preservation of the original word order at 15:12d.

Characteristics of 336.

There are 110 singular readings of 336. There are thirty-two spelling changes, of which the most common are variations in the length of the *o*-vowel, occurring ten times. Other spelling changes include itacism, the addition or omission of letters, and the exchange of vowels. The most common of the latter are between an *alpha* and *epsilon*, occurring three times. There are nine instances of apparent change in case due to scribal error. There are six changes in the number of a noun or a personal pronoun, of which five are grammatically incorrect. There are nine changes in verbs. In twenty-two cases, words and phrases are read by 336 which are omitted by other groups, including three additions by dittography. There are fifteen omissions in 336 of material found in other text types, including four large portions of text, three nouns, and five articles, of which three are followed in other text types by genitive personal pronouns. The latter omissions are characteristic of Greek which has been translated from semitic languages. There are several instances of substitution, including Ιερουσαλημ for Ισραηλ on three occasions, and three exchanges between θεος and κυριος. Several substitutions involve scribal emendations or the confusion of similarly-appearing uncial forms.

The twelve readings which 336 shares with the 253 group are described on page 92 above. The thirteen readings shared by 336 and the 260 group are described on page 93. There are sixteen readings shared by 336 and the 629 group. These readings, the converse of readings shared between the 253 and 260 groups, described on pages 87 and 88, include itacisms and other spelling variations, changes in case, and substitutions.

The following summarizes the textual characteristics of 336:

Characteristic:	alone	253	260	629
Verb changes	X			
Transpositions				
Omissions and additions	X		X	
Substitutions	X	X		X
Case changes	X			X
Spelling changes	X	X	X	X

(336 Combined with:)

There are six probable original readings or readings characteristic of an earlier stage in the text among the singular readings of 336. These include three instances at which the use of articles combined with following genitive personal pronouns has been avoided, and the substitutions at 9:6a, 9:6i, and 15:10c.

Characteristics of the 629 Group.

The two witnesses of the 629 group share twenty readings against those of the other text types. Four of these are spelling variations, of which two are derived from uncial forms. Two verb changes have occurred. In each of the latter the 629 group reads an indicative mood in contrast to the participle, infinitive, or subjunctive of the non-629 witnesses. There are three instances of additions in this text group and six cases of omissions. Two phrases have been omitted by

Text-type Characteristics 95

haplography. Two transpositions have occurred by error. In two cases a synonym or pronoun is used in place of κυριου, read by the other text groups.

The characteristics of the 629 group in combination with the other text groups have appeared in the preceding pages. Readings shared by the 629 and 253 groups and those shared by the 629 and 260 groups include spelling variations and substitutions. Readings found in 336 and the 629 group include spelling variations, changes in case, and substitutions.

The following graph summarizes the textual characteristics of the 629 group:

Characteristics:	629 alone	Combined with: 253	260	336
Verb changes	X			
Transpositions	X			
Omissions and additions	X	X		
Substitutions	X		X	X
Case changes				X
Spelling changes	X	X	X	X

There are no probable original readings or readings characteristic of early stages in the history of the text which are read by the 629 group alone.

The relationships among the *PssSol* text groups and the transmission of the textual tradition will be examined in the following chapter.

CHAPTER SIX

THE MANUSCRIPT HISTORY

The preceding chapters have presented a detailed analysis of the text of the *PssSol*. Chapter four analyzed the readings of the component witnesses of the 253, 260, and 629 text groups, described the textual characteristics of each MS, and established the relationships within each text group. Chapter five analyzed the readings of the representative witnesses of the text types, and described the characteristics of each. The present chapter will conclude the task of reconstructing the manuscript history by investigating what can be known from the witnesses about the history of the transmission of the text. The chapter will conclude by discussing the implications of this study for further investigation of the text of the *PssSol*.

RECONSTRUCTING THE MANUSCRIPT HISTORY

The study to be undertaken in this chapter recalls Westcott and Hort's famous dictum: "All trustworthy restoration of corrupted texts is founded on the study of their history."[1] It will be the task of the present section to investigate what can be known about the history of the transmission of the text of the *PssSol* from the analysis of the readings of their several text types and the MSS of which they are composed. The initial steps toward the reconstruction of the MS history have already been taken in the previous chapters. The evidence from these chapters will be employed in the present section.

Von Gebhardt's Stemma.

Von Gebhardt established what he believed to be the genetic relationship among the witnesses of the *PssSol* by means of demonstrating the antiquity of the readings preserved in MS 253 and then relating the other witnesses to 253 on the basis of the extent of agreement and disagreement of each MS with the readings of 253. Von Gebhardt concluded that 253 represents the most reliable text of the *PsSol* on the basis of a comparison of its stylistic characteristics with those of the oldest Greek biblical MSS. These features include the use of the final *nu*, the preference of ειπον to ειπα, and the use of sigmatic aorist endings.[2] Each of these characteristics has been observed in the preceding chapter.

Von Gebhardt located the other witnesses in terms of their apparent relationship to 253. Since 336 has a high number of agreements with 253, he concluded that a close relationship exists between these MSS: "Dass R und J einander nahe stehen, ist hiernach zweifellos."[3] This accords with the findings of the preceding chapter, in which several readings shared by the 253 group and 336 were found to be characteristic of early MSS or probable original readings.[4] The textual ancestor of 336, according to von Gebhardt, is an uncial MS in the chain of transmission between the archetype of all extant witnesses and the 260-629 text groups. This ancestor is represented in von Gebhardt's stemma, reproduced on page 35 above, by a lower case *x*. The 260 and 629 groups are descended from this MS through a common ancestor *w*. The no longer extant minuscule MSS *v* and *u* stand between *w* and the 629 and 260 groups, respectively.[5] The fact that 629 and 769 are descended from a common ancestor has been established in chapter four. That the later members of the 260 group, 471, 606, and 3004, are descended from 149-260 has also been demonstrated. It is not possible to determine with assurance, however, that 260 and not 149 is the ancestral MS of 471-606.

It will be recalled from the preceding chapter that fifty readings which are probable original readings or readings typical of older witnesses are found in the 253 group, that six are found in 336, and that only two are found in the 260 group. The 629 preserves such readings only in combinations with other text types. While these proportions of early or original readings may be accounted for satisfactorily by von Gebhardt's stemma, there remain other considerations which must be explained. It has been seen that the 253 group and 336 agree in twelve readings against the other text groups. Eleven readings, an almost equal number, are shared by the 253 and 260 groups, and thirteen are shared by the 253 and 629 text groups. If the

Manuscript History 99

MS groups of the *PssSol* are related in the way von Gebhardt's stemma indicates, one would expect a relatively high number of shared readings between the 253 group and 336, since they are related by a near ancestor, and fewer between the 253 group and the 260 or 629 group, since each of these is separated from the 253 group by several additional copyings. One must therefore explain how the 253 group shares with the 260 and 629 groups a number of readings which is, on the average, the same as it shares with its nearer relative 336.

There can be only two satisfactory explanations for these readings within the framework of von Gebhardt's genealogy. Either 336 and its partner have independently and identically deviated from their received text, which has been preserved by 253 and its partner, or they have correctly preserved the reading of their received text against the reading of 253, but the remaining text type has independently restored the reading of 253. In sum, if von Gebhardt's analysis is to stand, shared readings of this nature must be found to be coincidental and without genetic significance.[6]

There are indeed several readings which are capable of being explained in this way. The omission of the final *nu* by 336 and the 629 group at 1:5cd, for example, may be simultaneous alterations following the later practice, and need not have genetic significance. A similar case is the agreement between the 253 and 260 groups at 2:14, where the latter has corrected the spelling error of its received text, and thereby coincidentally created a shared reading with the 253 group. Other shared readings which yield to the explanation of coincidence are those between the 253 and 260 groups at 2:9a, 2:14a, 2:21b, 8:33g, and 18:9b, and between the 253 and 629 groups at 2:8a, 2:31a, 3:1a, 4:8d, 4:10c, and 17:9c.

Other readings exist, however, which cannot be as readily explained as coincidental agreements or as restorations by another text type of the reading of the 253 group. Examples include the readings of the 260 group at 8:34b and 15:12d, which were identified in chapter five as probable original readings. For these to be original readings in von Gebhardt's stemma, the agreement of the non-260 groups must be explained as identical and coincidental departures from the received text.

Another example is the words εν απασι, read by the 253 and 629 groups at 4:21c. The use of απας after a vowel accords with the usual practice in the LXX and in Ptolemaic Greek.[7] The less common reading of 336 and the 260 group is therefore the probable original reading.[8] It is unlikely that the 253-629 group readings represent coincidental scribal alterations to the text, since these have not changed the similar reading τουτων απαντων at 13:4. Another example is the shared reading of 336 and the 629 group πολυν for πολλην at 1:3c. For this agreement to be coincidental, as von Gebhardt's analysis must conclude, both itacism and the omission of a *lambda* must have occurred simultaneously in two independent copyings.[9] Another example is the reading of 336 and the 629 group at 15:7e, θειων for οσιων. While the original variation is attributable to a misreading in an uncial text, θειων is not an uncommon word in the LXX, and would have presented no difficulties to a subsequent scribe such as to have caused the substitution of another word. A similar case is the substitution shared by the 253 and 260 groups at 10:8cd.

The solution to the foregoing is not to be sought by demonstrating that each of these examples can be fit into von Gebhardt's stemma. This can in fact be done, in most instances by assuming that identical but coincidental variations have taken place. The effect of these instances, however, should be to recall the principle that that explanation is best which accounts for the evidence with the fewest necessary supporting assumptions. These instances are, in the language of T. Kuhn's The Structure of Scientific Revolutions, anomalies requiring the adjustment or abandonment of the received paradigm. An alternative explanation of the shared readings of the *PssSol* must be sought, which does not require frequent reliance on the assumption of coincidence.

An alternative explanation is suggested by the recognition of the extent to which textual mixture has occurred in ancient biblical MSS. Sidney Jellicoe refers to "the 'mixed' nature of even the oldest and 'best' of our manuscripts", and concludes that this and other phenomena "strongly suggest that our system of grouping is perchance too narrow and has failed to take

Manuscript History   101

account of the possibility of additional recensions in quite early times."[10] Bruce Metzger has written the following:

A disturbing element enters when mixture has occurred, that is, when a copyist has had two or more manuscripts before him and has followed sometimes one, sometimes the other; or, as sometimes happened, when a scribe copied a manuscript from one exemplar and corrected it against another. To the extent that manuscripts have a 'mixed' ancestry, the genealogical relations among them become progressively more complex and obscure to the investigator.[11]

When the possibility of textual mixture and of additional recensions in the transmission of the text is taken into account, a genealogy different from that of von Gebhardt is suggested: The 253 group and 336 represent ancient traditions of the text of the *PssSol*. Each of these text types preserves, both in readings shared by both and in readings unique to each, the most ancient and reliable readings of the *PssSol* available in the extant witnesses. The remaining groups are descended from a mixed text which has incorporated readings from the 253 group and 336. In addition, there was available to the copyist of the 260 tradition another textual tradition which was the source of the two probable original readings preserved by that text group.

The Transmission of the Text.

The genealogy described in the preceding paragraph may be put in graphic form as follows:

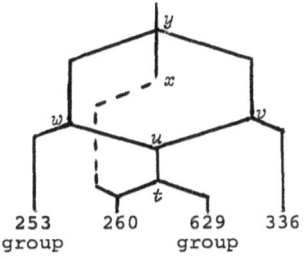

253   260   629   336
group   group

In this stemma, y is the archetype of the extant *PssSol* text types. This is similar to the y of von Gebhardt's stemma. The uncial ancestors of the 253 group and 336, respectively, are w and v. The common ancestor of the 260 and 629 groups is t, similar to von Gebhardt's w. This MS is a descendant from the mixed text u. The recension which was available to the copyist of the 260 tradition is represented by x. The broken line between x and the 260 group represents the relatively small dependence of the latter upon this recension.

This genealogy allows the readings of the *PssSol* witnesses to be explained in the following manner: Readings shared by the 253 group and 336 are derived from their ancestor y. Readings at which the 260 and 629 groups agree against the 253 group and 336 originated in the transmission between u and t. Since the 260 and 629 groups share readings derived from an uncial stage in the transmission of the text, u is shown to have been an uncial MS. Singular readings of the 629 group represent departures from the text of t. Since no singular readings of this group have been shown to be early or probable original readings, no further pursuit of the origin of these readings is necessary. Singular readings of the 260 group are also departures from the text of t. Since, however, the readings at 8:34b and 15:12d have been identified as probable original readings, it must be explained how these readings came to the 260 group. The explanation lies in the use of the 260 group not only of the text of t, but also of the no longer extant x recension. By means of this recension the 260 group has preserved two original readings not found in the other text types.

The hypothesis of the x recension allows the phenomena of shared readings to be explained. Where the 253 and 260 groups share readings against 336 and the 629 group, the w and x texts have agreed against v, the reading of the mixed text u has followed v, and 260 has departed from v in favor of the x recension. Where the agreement is between the 253 and 629 groups against the 260 group and 336, the x and v traditions have agreed against w, u has copied from w, and 260 has again followed the x recension. Each of these patterns of shared readings is caused by a departure of w or v from the received

Manuscript History 103

text, with u copying from the minority and 260 following x. That only these specific combinations could have produced the patterns of shared readings under discussion accounts for the relative infrequency of these readings in a book in which over four hundred instances of variation among the component text types have been observed.[12] The 260 group has followed the x recension against the readings of t twenty-six times.[13]

It will be noted that the above paradigm, which posits textual mixture and the use by the 260 group of a no longer extant recension, allows all combinations of variant readings among the $PssSol$ text types to be explained without requiring the frequent assumption of coincidence in accounting for the shared readings.

It is useful at this juncture to summarize the conclusions which were reached in chapter four concerning the relationships of the MSS within the 253, 260, and 629 text groups. There are several stages in the transmission of the text within the 253 group. The present MSS of this group are derived from a no longer extant uncial ancestor. MS 253 is a close copy of this text. The other witnesses, 655 and 659, are copies of an exemplar which is related to MS 253 by means of the common group ancestor. The immediate ancestor of the 260 group is the present MS 260. From this witness, 149 was made as an almost identical copy. The remaining MSS of this group are descended from a copy of either 149 or 260.[14] MSS 471 and 606 are related by means of a common ancestor, from which they were indirectly copied. MSS 471 and 3004 are related more closely through a MS common to each. The members of the 629 group, MSS 629 and 769, are related through an ancestor in the chain of tradition between them and the other text groups.

It is now possible to complete the diagram of the relationships among the text groups by including the stemmata of the relationships of the witnesses within each text group:

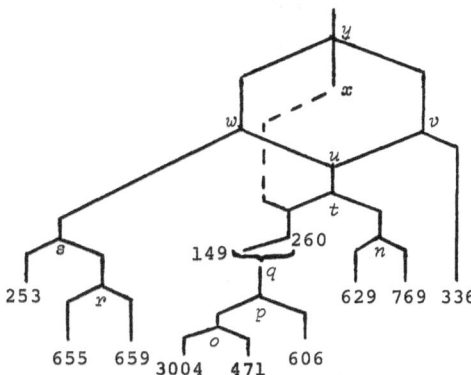

The letter s represents the common ancestor to the 253 group, and r the ancestor to 655-659. The immediate copy of 149 or 260 is designated q. The horizontal bracket below 149 and 260 denotes the uncertainty as to which of these MSS was in fact the exemplar for q. The immediate common ancestor of the remaining witnesses of the 260 group is p. The common ancestor of 471 and 3004 is o. The remaining symbol, n, is the common ancestor of MSS 629 and 769 within the 629 group. Of these symbols, p represents the same MS as von Gebhardt's h, and n the same MS as his v. This stemma is intended to express the genetic relationships among the witnesses of the $PsSol$. The vertical position of the MSS does not indicate the relative date of their composition.

With the exception of the transcription of some of the extant MSS, it is not possible to assign specific historical or geographic provenances to the stages in the above genealogy. There is evidence, however, that the text of the $PsSol$ was preserved in some form into the middle ages in Byzantine libraries. Reference has been made in chapter one to marginal notations in MS 253 which indicate that this witness was owned by a private individual in a Greek-speaking area. In addition, 260 and 606 were observed to have existed in Constantinople.

Manuscript History   105

The most likely place for the preservation of the psalms may be
the monasteries of Mt. Athos: MSS 336 and 471 are from the
Iberon monastery on Mt. Athos, and 769 is from the Laura monastery, some twenty miles distant. The possibility that the
PssSol were preserved on Mt. Athos is enhanced by the fact that
these MSS represent three of the four *PssSol* text types. In
addition, it is known that the monasteries of Mt. Athos had
among the largest collections of MSS in the Byzantine world.
A nineteenth-century estimate was that two thousand MSS were at
the Iberon library and that nine hundred were in the library at
the Laura monastery.[15] It may be that more MSS of the *PssSol*
existed at Mt. Athos: major removals of the possessions of the
monasteries occurred during the Fourth Crusade in the thirteenth
century before the monasteries of Mt. Athos were taken under
the protection of the emperor and the pope.[16] Other MSS were
taken from the monasteries or destroyed during the fifteenth
to eighteenth centuries.[17] The cataloguing of the MSS of Mt.
Athos may still be incomplete.[18]

RECONSTRUCTING THE TEXT

With the conclusion of the preceding section, the objective of the present study was reached. It will be recalled
that the purpose of this work, as stated in its introduction is
as follows: "It is the objective of the present work to undertake a thorough examination of the relationships among the
readings of the MSS of the *PssSol* and to reconstruct the genealogy of the extant witnesses." This having been accomplished,
however, it is appropriate to address briefly the matter to
which these conclusions are most likely to be applied: the
reconstruction of the text of the *PssSol*. This section will
apply the conclusions which have been reached in this study to
the question of method for the textual criticism of the *PssSol*.

The Evidence of Genealogy and the Documents.

A first basis for evaluating the readings is provided by
the genealogical conclusions of this study, which indicate which
MSS are the best representatives of the several text types and

which text types are the most likely to have preserved the archetypical text of the *PssSol*.[19] The genetic relationships within each of the text types has been summarized on pages 118-119. The ancestor of the 253 group was the archetype of both MS 253 and the common ancestor of 655 and 659. This text is represented in this work by readings shared by MS 253 and one other member of the 253 text group. It is unlikely that a reading found only in 655 or 659 would be an original reading, since in this eventuality the reading of 253 and the other MS of the group would have to have been independent and coincidental agreements. MS 260 has been shown to be the ancestral MS of the 260 text group, and has been used to represent this group throughout the present study. Since 260 is the ancestor of 471-606-3004, readings of these, whether singular or in combination, which are not also read by 149-260, cannot be original readings.[20] The ancestor of the 629 group was similar to the present MSS 629 and 769 without the changes in wording of the former and the spelling variations of the latter. This text has been represented by readings shared by 629 and 769.

The stemma which appeared above was based on the observed patterns of relationships among the readings of the witnesses. The relative reliability of the text types may be inferred from this genealogy. The 253 group and 336 each preserve readings from an ancient recension of the *PssSol*. The 629 group is descended from a mixed text which combined readings from the 253 and 336 text traditions. Since the 629 group has had available to it no other sources of readings, readings found only in that group must be subsequent scribal variations, and cannot be considered to be original readings of the *PssSol*. The 260 group is descended from the same mixed text as 629, but has also utilized readings from another recension which is no longer extant. The 260 group has received twenty-six readings from this recension, including two probable original readings.

A further basis for the reconstruction of the text is documentary evidence: evidence of the general reliability of each witness as that reliability is discovered by means of an examination of its readings.[21] In order to discuss the reliability of the MSS of the *PssSol*, it is useful to summarize briefly the characteristics of the witnesses and text groups as

Manuscript History   107

they were identified in the previous two chapters. All witnesses and groups display spelling variations. Each text group is distinguished from others by spelling changes, some of which are derived from uncial forms. The spelling which is characteristic of the 253 group preserves the final *nu* found in older MSS; this characteristic is also found in 769. A frequent spelling phenomenon of MS 471 is the omission of initial letters.

In addition to spelling variations, the 253 group members 655 and 659 have been seen to be characterized by haplography, dittography, intentional substitutions, and other attempts to produce a smoother text. The 253 group readings display several grammatical characteristics of an early stage in the text, including the use of sigmatic aorist endings and the avoidance of the article with a following genitive personal pronoun. The representative witness of the 260 group, MS 260, preserves two probable original readings together with substitutions and additions in the interest of a smoother text. The latter are also characteristic of 471, 606, and 3004, the later members of this group. MS 336 preserves a distinct text type. Its characteristics include grammatical errors, intentional and unintentional substitutions, additions, and omissions. The 629 group is made up of the MSS 629 and 769. When contrasted to 769, 629 has avoided numerous spelling errors, but has introduced several substitutions and other changes in wording, and so is a less reliable witness than 769 to the text of the common exemplar. The 629 group readings are characterized by omissions and substitutions and other changes in wording.

The different variations described above are not of equal value for determining the reliability of a witness. Readings, as well as MSS, must be weighed and not counted. The least significant readings for evaluating witnesses are spelling variations. Not only are spelling variations among the most common of scribal changes, they are in most cases easily identifiable, and should not alter that estimate of a witness's reliability which would otherwise prevail.[22] It is on this basis that 769, although possessing many spelling errors, may be concluded to be a more reliable witness than its partner 629, which avoids spelling errors but introduces changes in wording.

In any event, the search for the original spelling of a text may be futile: fixed orthography had not yet come into existence in the first centuries of the Common Era.[23] With regard to spelling, the textual critic can only follow the practice of the editors of Shakespeare by adopting a spelling consistent with early usage without assuming that the spelling of the author has thereby been reproduced.

Once spelling variations are omitted from consideration, it becomes possible on the basis of the descriptions of the textual characteristics of the witnesses and text groups to identify those MSS whose readings are more typical of later than of earlier stages in the transmission of the text or which reflect common scribal errors, and to exclude these from consideration as reliable witnesses to the text of the *PsSol*.[24] Characteristics of later witnesses include the substitution of a more common for a less familiar term, the addition of complements such as articles and conjunctions, and other attempts to render the text more intelligible or stylistically more acceptable.[25] Common scribal errors include erroneous transpositions and additions or omissions by dittography or haplography.[26] The frequent occurrence of these characteristics in a MS, in the absence of probable original readings, should render singular readings of that MS as unlikely candidates for consideration as original readings. On this basis, readings which are found only in 471, 606, 629, 655, 659, 769, or 3004 as singular readings of these MSS are not likely to be original readings of the *PsSol*.[27]

An additional basis for arriving at an evaluation of the witnesses may be found in observing the frequency of the occurrence in each MS of probable original readings or readings characteristic of an early stage in the transmission of the text. It will be recalled from the preceding chapter that fifty such readings were found among the singular readings of the 253 group, two among the readings of the 260 group, and six among the readings of 336. No probable original readings were found among the singular readings of the 629 group. These groups may therefore be ranked in the following order in terms of the probability that a singular reading of each preserves an original reading of the *PssSol*: the 253 group, 336, the 260 group, and the 629 group.[28]

A greater inherent probability resides in readings supported by two text types. Of these, the most reliable shared readings are likely to be those found in the 253 group and 336, followed by readings of the former and the 260 group. Since the 629 group readings have been shown to be derived from a mixture of the 253 and 336 text traditions, an agreement of the 629 group with either of these cannot add weight to the reading in question. An agreement of the 629 group with the 260 group against the 253 group and 336 cannot be an original reading, since shared 260-629 group readings can only have originated as subsequent departures from the ancestral mixed text.[29] Since singular readings of the 629 group can have originated only by error, readings of three groups against the 629 group have a virtual certainty of being correct.[30] Readings at which the 629 group supports the text of two other groups against a fourth are not made more reliable by the added testimony of the 629 group, since the text of the latter in such cases can only have been derived from the 253 or 336 recension and so offers no additional substantiation to the readings.[31]

The Internal Evidence of Readings.

It should be clear from a review of the preceding chapters that genealogical and documentary considerations alone cannot solve the textual problems of the *PssSol*. Although, for instance, there is a high inherent probability of originality residing in readings supported by the 253 group and 336 against the 260 group, two singular readings of the latter have been identified as probable original readings.[32] Genealogical and documentary evidence, therefore, cannot by themselves establish the text of the *PssSol*, and must be combined with the internal evidence of readings.

The internal evidence of readings is customarily divided into intrinsic and transcriptional probability. Intrinsic probability refers to considerations of what the author was more likely to have written. Transcriptional probability refers to the consideration of what changes were more likely to have been introduced by subsequent copyists. There is necessarily a balance to be sought between these two considerations. Westcott and Hort note that a reading which appears to be the "best" may not have originated with the author.[33] Examples of this ambiguity are LXX allusions in the *PsSol* which, on intrinsic grounds, may be assumed to have been the creation of the original writer, since such allusions are found frequently in the *PsSol*. When, however, some witnesses preserve a text in which the allusion does not appear, the transcriptional considerations outweigh the intrinsic considerations, since it is more likely that a Septuagintal allusion was created by a copyist than that an original allusion was removed from the text by the scribe of the opposing tradition.[34]

Intrinsic considerations may be applied with the greatest certainty when a reading displays grammatical or other features which can be dated with assurance to the early stages in the transmission of the text. Several of these features are displayed in the 253 group readings, and include the use of sigmatic aorist endings, the retention of the final *nu*, and the avoidance of articles attached to nouns with following genitive personal pronouns. In these cases intrinsic and transcriptional factors coincide, since it is unlikely that any of these would have been introduced into the text by a copyist accustomed to a later Greek style. Other factors in weighing intrinsic probability are the style and vocabulary of the author throughout a work and the usage of the immediate context.[35] The latter consideration was used to determine the original reading at *PsSol* 10:8cd.

The most useful canon of transcriptional probability is the principle that the more difficult reading is more likely to be original. The application of this principle may be guided by Metzger's summary of common scribal emendations:

> Scribes would sometimes (a) replace an unfamiliar word with a more familiar synonym, (b) alter a less refined grammatical form or less elegant lexical expression in accord with Atticizing preferences, or (c) add pronouns, conjunctions, and expletives to make a smooth text.[36]

The more difficult reading is that reading more likely to have been altered by a scribe: "Intrinsic inferiority is evidence of originality."[37] There are, however, instances

Manuscript History   111

where a reading becomes so difficult that it could only have
originated by scribal error: one must assume that the text was
intelligible to its original readers.[38] It is unlikely that
the readings of 655 at 9:7c, 14:3b, and 15:8f, to select three
examples, were written by the original author.

One may find in the *PssSol* examples of all three categories of the scribal emendations named by Metzger in the preceding paragraph. Among the many instances where a less
familiar word has been replaced by a more common term, the
readings of 336 at 4:16e and 9:6a, and of the 260 and 629 groups
at 17:41b may be cited as examples. Examples of scribal alterations in the interest of grammatical or lexical improvement
are the readings of the non-253 groups against the 253 group
in the use of nonsigmatic aorist endings, and the substitution
by 336 at 3:10d. There are many instances of the addition of
complementary words to produce improved readings: examples are
the readings of the 253 group at 2:25a, 2:32a, 3:11a, 3:12a,
and 17:30c, and of the 260 group at 4:15b, 5:11a, 11:1c, 11:8,
14:5c, and 15:12a. In each of these instances the evidence of
transcriptional probability has been used to determine the
probable original reading.

The Textual Criticism of the Psalms of Solomon.

An important implication of the foregoing, which is appli-
cable not only to the *PssSol* but also to other literature of
the Pseudepigrapha of the Old Testament, is that the detailed
examination of textual evidence, which is assumed as a matter
of course to be necessary when dealing with the LXX or the NT,
is no less necessary when one is dealing with a writing which
is not a part of the Jewish or Christian canons,[39] and which is
preserved in only a few witnesses.

The establishment of the text of the *PssSol* should pro-
ceed in the order indicated in the present chapter: with first
consideration to genealogical and documentary evidence.[40]
There can be no value in discussing the intrinsic or transcriptional probabilities inherent in a reading of a given MS, if
that witness has already been shown to be a poor copy of an
inferior exemplar. The effect of genealogical and documentary

evidence for establishing the text of the *PssSol* is both positive and negative. The positive contribution of this evidence is the identification of certain text types as preserving readings from ancient forms of the *PssSol* text. These readings have been preserved most frequently in the 253 group. Since the ancestral text of this group is no longer extant, the group is most reliably represented by readings found in both MS 253 and either 655 or 659. Ancient readings are also found, although much less frequently, in MS 336. Early readings can also be found in the 260 group when that group has departed from the mixed text it shares with the 629 group as a common ancestor, and follows its own textual tradition.

The negative conclusion of genealogical and documentary evidence is to identify other MSS as unreliable witnesses to the text of the *PssSol*. These are 471, 606, and 3004, since they are derived from 149-260 and can add no additional attestation to the original text of this group; and 629 and 769, since they are descended from a mixture of the 253 and 336 text traditions and can contain distinctive readings only by departing from their received text. In each of these cases, no additional weight is added to a reading by the support of these witnesses, and their singular readings are to be rejected.[41] Readings shared by 655 and 659 against 253 are derived from their common ancestor, and may preserve original group readings.[42] Such instances must be evaluated on the basis of internal evidence. A singular reading of 655 or 659 against the other group members is extremely unlikely to be an original reading, since in this case the agreement of the remaining members of the group would have to be coincidental.

IMPLICATIONS FOR FURTHER STUDY

The task of the present work, as defined in the first chapter, is completed by the establishment of the methodological guidelines described in the preceding section. It is useful, however, to describe the following implications and areas for further research.

Manuscript History   113

*The Textual Relationship of the Psalms of Solomon to Other
Writings in the Manuscripts.*

Six of the eleven MSS of the *PsSol* also contain the
Wisdom of Solomon and Sirach: 149, 253, 260, 336, 471, and 606.
These writings have received far more attention than have the
PsSol, and have a more firmly established textual history.[43]
In each of these except 336, the *PsSol* appear between Wisdom
and Sirach. The 253 text of the latter writings has been identified as preserving the hexaplaric recension which originated
with Origen in the third century.[44] The MSS of the 260 group
also form a text group in Wisdom and Sirach, which is often
related to the Lucianic recension.[45] The inference is tempting
that these *PsSol* text types are genetically related to the
text groups which the same MSS represent in Wisdom and Sirach.
If this were the case, it would be possible to identify as
hexaplaric the 253 text of the *PsSol* and as Lucianic the tradition which has been sometimes employed by the 260 group.
The testing of this inference must await a detailed examination
and comparison of the textual characteristics of these groups
not only in the *PsSol* but also in Wisdom and Sirach.[46]

The Syrohexaplar and the Syriac Text of the Psalms of Solomon.

This consideration is related to the foregoing. The 253
text of Wisdom and Sirach, as has been stated above, is hexaplaric. An important witness to the hexaplaric recension is
the Syrohexaplar, a translation into Syriac of the fifth column
of Origen's Hexapla.[47] Since Begrich has demonstrated that
close connections exist between the Greek text of MS 253 and
the Syriac MSS of the *PsSol*,[48] it is possible that the existing
Syriac text of the *PsSol* may also be hexaplaric. If either
this or the foregoing were true, the 253 text of the *PsSol*
could be identified as having preserved the hexaplaric recension.[49]

114   Psalms of Solomon

Geographical and Historical Factors in the Manuscript Tradition.

It has been suggested above that the Greek text of the Psalms may have been preserved into the middle ages in the monasteries of Mt. Athos. It would be useful for a more complete reconstruction of the transmission history if the geographical and historical factors in the MS tradition were more fully explored. This would have immediate text-critical value, and could aid in identifying the ancient textual traditions of the *PsSol*.

The Textual Criticism of Other Writings of the Pseudepigrapha of the Old Testament.

The specific conclusions reached in the present work concerning the groups, witnesses, and readings of the *PsSol* can apply, of course, only to that writing. The same detailed investigation of the text, however, has yet to be done for many of the other writings which resemble the *PsSol* in being preserved in a relatively few witnesses and excluded from the canon.[50] While it may be assumed that the methodological principles described in the present chapter may be useful with regard to other Greek writings, the specific applicability of these principles will be evident only after a similar examination of their textual situations has been made.[51]

NOTES TO INTRODUCTION

[1] MS 3004 divides *PsSol* 18, forming a nineteenth Psalm following 18:9.

[2] A.-M. Denis, *Introduction aux Pseudépigraphes grecs d'Ancien Testament* (Leiden: Brill, 1970), p. 64; Leonhard Rost, *Einleitung in die alttestamentlichen Apokryphen und Pseudepigraphen* (Heidelberg: Quelle & Meyer, 1971), pp. 89-91.

[3] A. Dupont-Sommer, *The Essene Writings of Qumran* (Cleveland: Meridian, 1966), pp. 296, 337; R. Wright, "The Psalms of Solomon, the Pharisees, and the Essenes," *1972 Proceedings*, International Organization for Septuagint and Cognate Studies (Missoula, Mont.: Scholars Press, 1972), pp. 146-147.

[4] Their concern for the purity of the temple is an example: see 2:2-5.

[5] The separatism of 17:17 is characteristic of the Essenes.

[6] S. Sandmel has declared that until new archaeological evidence is discovered, "it would be useful for scholarship to declare a moratorium on the search for precise history." *The First Christian Century in Judaism and Christianity* (New York: Oxford, 1969), p. 158.

[7] A. Rahlfs, ed., *Septuaginta*, 7th edition, vol 2 (Stuttgart: Württembergische Bibelanstalt, 1935), pp. 471-489.

[8] The method is described briefly by Eldon Jay Epp, "The Claremont Profile-Method for Grouping New Testament Minuscule Manuscripts," in *Studies in the History and Text of the New Testament*, ed. by B. L. Daniels and M. J. Suggs (Salt Lake City: University of Utah Press, 1967), pp. 27-38. A detailed description of the CPM will appear in Chapter three below.

NOTES TO CHAPTER ONE

[1] A. Rahlfs, *Verzeichnis der griechischen Handschriften des Alten Testaments* (Göttingen: K. Gesellschaft der Wissenschaften, 1914); Oscar von Gebhardt used the following letter symbols for the MSS: V = 149, R = 253, K = 260, I = 336, M = 471, P = 606, C = 629, and L = 769. (*Die Psalmen Salomo's* [Leipzig: J. C. Hinrichs'sche Buchhandlung, 1895]).

[2] Rahlfs, *Verzeichnis*, p. 318.

[3] J. Ziegler, ed., *Sapientia Salomonis* (Göttingen: Vandenhoeck & Ruprecht, 1962), p. 8; *Sapientia Iesu Filii Sirach* (Göttingen: Vandenhoeck & Ruprecht, 1965), p. 7.

[4] Rahlfs, *Verzeichnis*, p. 249; von Gebhardt, *Psalmen*, p. 26.

[5] Rahlfs, *Verzeichnis*, p. 249.

[6] Ziegler, *Sapientia Salomonis*, p. 8; *Sirach*, p. 7.

[7] As observed by Rahlfs, *Verzeichnis*, p. 249.

[8] The Greek text is reproduced by von Gebhardt, *Psalmen*, p. 27.

[9] Rahlfs, *Verzeichnis*, p. 91.

[10] Ziegler, *Sapientia Salomonis*, p. 9; *Sirach*, p. 7.

[11] Rahlfs, *Verzeichnis*, p. 91.

[12] Von Gebhardt, *Psalmen*, p. 19.

[13] Ibid., p. 13.

[14] The lacuna consists of 35 verses. The six pages immediately preceding and following the lacuna contain, on the average, seven or eight verses per page. The 35 missing verses would have occupied four pages, comprising one folded leaf.

[15] For a collation of this fragment, see R. B. Wright and R. R. Hann, "A New Fragment of the Greek Text of Sirach," *JBL* 94:1 (1975) pp. 111-112. Ryle and James had earlier suggested that a leaf might have disappeared from the end of the archetype of the extant MSS of the *PssSol*: H. E. Ryle and M. R. James, *The Psalms of the Pharisees, Commonly Called the Psalms of Solomon* (Cambridge: University Press, 1891), pp. xxv, 149.

Notes to pp. 4-6

[16] Ziegler, *Sapientia Salomonis*, p. 9; *Sirach*, p. 7.

[17] Von Gebhardt, *Psalmen*, p. 16; Rahlfs, *Verzeichnis*, p. 145.

[18] Rahlfs, *Verzeichnis*, p. 145.

[19] Ziegler, *Sapientia Salomonis*, p. 9; *Sirach*, p. 7.

[20] Rahlfs, *Verzeichnis*, p. 234.

[21] Ibid., p. 213.

[22] Ziegler, *Sapientia Salomonis*, p. 10; *Sirach*, p. 7.

[23] Von Gebhardt, *Psalmen*, p. 29; Rahlfs, *Verzeichnis*, p. 234.

[24] Rahlfs, *Verzeichnis*, p. 234.

[25] Von Gebhardt, *Psalmen*, p. 30.

[26] There are large areas where the text appears to have been damaged by a spill or other discoloration. These areas are not mentioned by von Gebhardt, and so may have been damaged after his collation was made.

[27] Rahlfs, *Verzeichnis*, p. 240.

[28] Ibid., p. 241.

[29] Ibid., p. 20.

[30] According to information contained in a letter of June 28, 1973, from E. Hadjidakis, the director of the Benaki Museum, MS 769 was stolen from Laura around the turn of the century, and was acquired by the museum in 1931.

[31] Von Gebhardt, *Psalmen*, p. 29; Rahlfs, *Verzeichnis*, p. 20.

[32] Rahlfs, *Verzeichnis*, p. 20.

[33] Ibid., p. 95. A letter of July 7, 1976, from R. Hanhart, the director of the Septuaginta-Unternehmen der Akademie der Wissenschaften in Göttingen, states that the designation 3004 was assigned to this MS.

[34] Rahlfs, *Verzeichnis*, p. 95; W. Baars, "A New Fragment of the Greek Version of the Psalms of Solomon", *VT* 11 (1961) p. 441.

[35] Rahlfs, *Verzeichnis*, p. 95.

[36] Baars, "Fragment," p. 441.

[37] Denis, *Introduction*, p. 63; Rost, *Einleitung*, p. 89.

[38] Syriac texts of the *PssSol* have been published by the following: J. R. Harris, *The Odes and Psalms of Solomon* (Cambridge: University Press, 1909); J. R. Harris and Alphonse Mingana, *The Odes and Psalms of Solomon* (Manchester: University Press, 1916); and W. Baars, *Psalms of Solomon* (Leiden: Brill, 1972).

[39] J. Viteau, *Les Psaumes de Salomon* (Paris: Letouzey et Ané, 1911), pp. 192-239.

[40] Denis, *Introduction*, pp. xi-xvi, 60; Ryle and James, *Psalms*, pp. xxi-xxvii.

[41] A photograph of this page may be found in *Codex Alexandrinus* (London: British Museum, 1915); the page is discussed by T. Zahn, *Geschichte des neutestamentlichen Kanons*, vol 2 (Erlangen: A. Deichert'sche Verlagsbuchhandlung, 1890), pp. 288-289.

[42] J. Rendel Harris, "Notes on the Sinaitic and Vatican Codices," *Johns Hopkins University Circular* 29 (March, 1884) p. 54. Denis (*Introduction*, p. 62) cites Zahn (*Geschichte*, p. 289) in support of his suggestion that the *PssSol* were once contained in Sinaiticus. There is no reference to Sinaiticus on the page cited, nor does there appear to be a dicussion of the original contents of the codex anywhere in Zahn's work.

[43] Von Gebhardt, *Psalmen*, p. 1; Viteau, *Psaumes*, pp. 192-193.

[44] Juan Luis de la Cerda, "Psalterium Salomonis," appendix to his *Adversaria Sacra* (Lyon: n.p., 1626). This was a huge work of 187 chapters. See Ryle and James, *Psalms*, p. xiii.

[45] De la Cerda, "Psalterium Salomonis", p. 3; Viteau, *Psaumes*, p. 192.

[46] See Ryle and James, *Psalms*, pp. xxvii, xxviii. They concluded that it was unlikely that the Augustanus Codex was the same as MS 260: p. xxxvi.

[47] Ibid.

[48] Von Gebhardt, *Psalmen*, p. 7.

[49] De la Cerda, "Psalterium Salomonis," pp. 15-20.

[50] J. A. Fabricius, *Codex pseudepigraphus Veteris Testamenti* (Hamburg and Leipzig: n.p., 1713); see Ryle and James, *Psalms*, p. xiv, Viteau, *Psaumes*, p. 145.

[51] Fabricius, *Codex*, p. 973; Viteau, *Psaumes*, p. 195; von Gebhardt, *Psalmen*, p. 5. The existence of the codex had already been noted in catalogs: Ryle and James, *Psalms*, p. xxviii.

[52] A. Hilgenfeld, *Messias Judaeorum* (Leipzig: Fuesianus, 1869). Hilgenfeld had previously published the text in "Die Psalmen Salomo's und die Himmelfahrt des Moses", *ZWT* 11 (1868) pp. 133-168, 356. See von Gebhardt, *Psalmen*, p. 9.

[53] Hilgenfeld, *Messias*, pp. xi-xiii.

[54] Ibid., pp. 4-5; Ryle and James, *Psalms*, p. xvi.

[55] Hilgenfeld, *Messias*, p. xvii. See p. 5, where he dissents from de Lagarde's view to the contrary.

[56] E. E. Geiger, *Der Psalter Salomo's Herausgegeben und Erklärt* (Augsburg: n.p., 1871).

[57] O. F. Fritzsche, *Libri apocryphi Veteris Testamenti pseudepigraphi selecti* (Leipzig: F. A. Brockhaus, 1871).

[58] Ibid., p. xxv; see p. 571.

[59] Ibid., p. xxv.

[60] J. Wellhausen, *Die Pharisäer und die Sadducäer* (Greifswald: n.p., 1874).

[61] Ibid., pp. 133, 136-137.

[62] B. Pick, "The Psalter of Solomon," *Presbyterian Review*, 1883, pp. 775-813. Ryle and James were sharply critical of Pick's translation, and considered its primary value to be that of introducing the *PssSol* to a "fresh circle of students." Ryle and James, *Psalms*, p. xviii.

[63] Pick, "Psalter," pp. 777, 785n.

[64] Ryle and James, *Psalms*.

[65] Ibid., pp. xxvii-xxx.

[66]Ibid., p. xxxiv.

[67]Ibid., pp. lxxvii-lxxxvii.

[68]Ibid., pp. lxxxvii-lxxxix.

[69]Ibid., pp. 147-148.

[70]Baars, "New Fragment," p. 441.

[71]H. B. Swete, *The Old Testament in Greek According to the Septuagint*, vol. 3 (Cambridge: University Press, 1894), pp. xvi-xvii, 765-787.

[72]Ibid., p. 780 (ω); p. 781 (πολεμιου).

[73]H. B. Swete, *The Psalms of Solomon with the Greek Fragments of the Book of Enoch* (Cambridge: University Press, 1899), pp. v-vi.

[74]See M. de Jonge, *De Toekomstverwachting in de Psalmen van Salomo* (Leiden: Brill, 1965), p. 32.

[75]Ryle and James, *Psalms*, pp. xxvii-xxviii.

[76]Ibid., p. xxvii.

[77]Von Gebhardt, *Psalmen*, pp. 2-3.

[78]Ibid., pp. 4-6.

[79]Ibid., pp. 6-7. The letter from von Tiefenau cites the Vienna codex precisely by the library's designation. G. B. Gray's statement that Ryle and James' *A* (de la Cerda) is the "faulty seventeenth century copy" of the Copenhagen MS 260 is incorrect. Gray, "The Psalms of Solomon," *APOT* 2:625.

[80]Von Gebhardt, *Psalmen*, p. 8.

[81]Von Gebhardt's orientation is reflected in his subtitle: "Mit Benutzung der Athoshandschriften und des Codex Casanatensis." Ibid., p. i.

[82]Ibid., pp. 14, 24-25.

[83]Ibid., p. 19.

[84]Ibid., p. 23.

Notes to pp. 9-11   121

[85]Ibid., pp. 30-32.

[86]Ibid., pp. 33-37.

[87]Ibid., pp. 37-38.

[88]Ibid., p. 39; Viteau, *Psaumes*, p. 157, Gray, "Psalms," p. 626, Harris, *Odes and Psalms*, p. 44.

[89]These MS groupings will be confirmed in chapter three below.

[90]Swete, *Psalms*.

[91]Harris, *Odes and Psalms*.

[92]Ibid., p. 42.

[93]Harris and Mingana, *Odes and Psalms*.

[94]Viteau, *Psaumes*.

[95]Gray, "Psalms," pp. 625-652.

[96]K. G. Kuhn, *Die älteste Textgestalt der Psalmen Salomos* (Stuttgart: W. Kohlhammer Verlag, 1937), pp. 8-17.

[97]Begrich, "Der Text der Psalmen Salomos," *ZNW* 38 (1939) pp. 131-164. Begrich's conclusion receives confirmation from the fact that the texts of Wisdom and Sirach in MS 253 are hexaplaric, with close connections to the Syrohexaplar. See J. Ziegler, "Die Hexaplarische Bearbeitung des griechischen Sirach," *BZ* N.F. 4 (1960) pp. 174-185.

[98]Wilhelm Pesch, "Die Abhängigkeit des 11. salomonischen Psalms von letzten Kapitel des Buches Baruch," *ZAW* 67 (1955) pp. 251-263.

[99]Baars, "New Fragment."

[100]De Jonge, *Toekomstverwachting*, pp. 18, 31, 37, 38. De Jonge believes the χριστος κυριος of 17:32 to be a Christian interpolation: p. 38.

[101]Wright and Hann, "New Fragment."

[102]Wright, "The Psalms of Solomon: a Provisional Collated Greek Text" (Philadelphia: Temple University, 1976).

[103] De Jonge, *Toekomstverwachting*, p. 32.

[104] Rahlfs, *Verzeichnis*, pp. 240, 241; Baars, "New Fragment."

[105] Von Gebhardt, *Psalmen*, pp. 15 (MS 149), 27 (MS 253), 16 (MSS 471 and 606).

[106] Ibid., pp. 14-15 (MS 260), 29 (MS 336), 30 (MS 629), 29 (MS 769).

[107] Ibid., p. 16.

[108] See above, p. 10.

[109] MSS 471 and 606 depart from 260 in the following instances: 4:15, 4:16, 5:1, 5:7, and 6:4. None of these are noted by von Gebhardt. It may be that, since 149-260-471-606 had been collated by Ryle and James in 1891 and by Swete in 1894, von Gebhardt believed that a full collation including these witnesses would be unnecessary.

NOTES TO CHAPTER TWO

[1] See C. Colwell, "The Greek New Testament with a Limited Critical Apparatus: Its Nature and Uses," in *Studies in New Testament and Early Christian Literature*, D. E. Aune, ed. (Leiden: Brill, 1972), pp. 31-40.

[2] See above, p. 10.

[3] O. von Gebhardt, *Die Psalmen Salomo's* (Leipzig: J. C. Hinrichs'sche Buchhandlung, 1895), p. 25.

[4] Von Gebhardt's reconstruction is designated "ego"; see for example p. 99.

[5] A. Rahlfs, ed., *Septuaginta* 7th edition, vol 2 (Stuttgart: Württembergische Bibelanstalt, 1935), p. 471.

[6] R. B. Wright, "The Psalms of Solomon, a Provisional Collated Greek Text: (Philadelphia: Temple University, 1976).

[7] Wright cites 3004 by the designation v and de la Cerda by A.

[8] Beck's collation was done while she was a graduate research assistant in the Department of Religion of Temple University in 1975. This collation has not been circulated, but was made available for use in the present project.

[9] Von Gebhardt, *Psalmen*, pp. 1-8.

[10] E. C. Colwell, *Studies in Methodology in Textual Criticism of the New Testament* (Grand Rapids: Eerdmans, 1969), pp. 57-58.

[11] The more complex superscriptions have a high probability of being later additions to the text. See B. M. Metzger, *The Text of the New Testament* (New York: Oxford University Press, 1968), pp. 26, 205.

[12] See, for instance, the usage of Rahlfs' *Septuaginta* and of Nestle's NT: E. Nestle, E. Nestle, and K. Aland, eds., *Novum Testamentum Graece* (Stuttgart: Württembergische Bibelanstalt, 1927.)

[13] Von Gebhardt, *Psalmen*, p. 96. Where the photographs are difficult to read they have been compared to von Gebhardt's collation.

[14] Von Gebhardt's reading: Ibid., p. 101.

[15] Von Gebhardt's reading: Ibid., p. 105.

[16] The text of 769 here and later in this verse has been badly obliterated. These obliterations appear to have been intentional, and have been corrected in a modern hand.

[17] Perhaps a misreading for ωκυδρομενους.

[18] Von Gebhardt, Psalmen, p. 23.

[19] R. B. Wright and R. R. Hann, "A New Fragment of the Greek Text of Sirach," JBL 94:1 (1975) pp. 111-112.

[20] MS 3004 forms an additional PsSol 19 from PsSol 18:10-12, under the superscription Ψαλμος τω Σαλομων Ιθ. See W. Baars, "A New Fragment of the Greek Version of the Psalms of Solomon," VT 11 (1961) p. 444.

NOTES TO CHAPTER THREE

[1] E. C. Colwell distinguishes among several types of text groups ("External Evidence and New Testament Textual Criticism," in *Studies in the History and Text of the New Testament*, B. E. Daniels and M. J. Suggs, eds. [Salt Lake City: University of Utah Press, 1967], pp. 9-15). Throughout the present work, "group" and "text type" will be used interchangeably, although, as will be seen, MS 336 forms a distinct text type.

[2] B. M. Metzger, *The Text of the New Testament* (New York: Oxford, 1968), p. 157.

[3] O. von Gebhardt, *Die Psalmen Salomo's* (Leipzig: J. C. Hinrichs'sche Buchhandlung, 1895), p. 39. In this representation, the letter designations used by von Gebhardt are replaced by the numerical designations of A. Rahlfs, *Verzeichnis der griechischen Handschriften des Alten Testaments* (Göttingen: K. Gesellschaft der Wissenschaften, 1914). See above, p. 2.

[4] Von Gebhardt, *Psalmen*, p. 32.

[5] Ibid., p. 38.

[6] Ibid., p. 39.

[7] Ibid., p. 23. See above, p. 10.

[8] Ibid., p. 39.

[9] Ibid.

[10] Ibid., p. 40.

[11] Throughout the present work, a group will be cited either by its constituent members, as 149-260-471-606, or by its archetypal or most prominent member, as the 260 group. Von Gebhardt uses the term *grupe* only of the 260 group. (*Psalmen*, p. 14) Although 629 and 769 share a common ancestor and distinguishing readings, von Gebhardt does not apply the term to these MSS. (Ibid., pp. 33-38) These witnesses qualify to be considered a group: See Colwell, "External Evidence," pp. 9-15.

[12] Von Gebhardt, *Psalmen*, pp. 42-46, 62-65.

[13] Ibid., pp. 33-34.

[14]E. J. Epp, "The Claremont Profile-Method for Grouping New Testament Minuscule Manuscripts" in *Studies in the History and Text of the New Testament*, B. E. Daniels and M. J. Suggs, eds. (Salt Lake City: University of Utah Press, 1967), p. 36. The Claremont Profile Method is designated CPM throughout the present work.

[15]E. C. Colwell, "The International Greek New Testament Project: a Status Report," *JBL* 87 (1968) pp. 191-197.

[16]P. R. McReynolds, "The Claremont Profile Method and the Grouping of Byzantine New Testament Manuscripts" (Ph.D. dissertation, Claremont Graduate School, 1968)

[17]F. Wisse, "The Claremont Profile Method for the Classification of Byzantine New Testament Manuscripts: a Study in Method" (Ph.D. dissertation, Claremont Graduate School, 1968)

[18]McReynolds, "CPM," p. 2. There were 1700 unclassified MSS.

[19]Wisse, "CPM," pp. 39-40: "Evidently there was less quality control in von Soden's offices than in a Byzantine scriptorium."

[20]Ibid., p. 72.

[21]Ibid., pp. 75-76.

[22]Ibid., pp. 83-84.

[23]Ibid., p. 79.

[24]McReynolds, "CPM," p. 4.

[25]Ibid.; Wisse, "CPM," p. 80.

[26]Ibid.

[27]Wisse, "CPM," p. 81.

[28]McReynolds, "CPM," pp. 4-5.

[29]Ibid., p. 5. Where the *textus receptus* reads τον λογον and one group of witnesses reads των λογων while another reads τους λογους, both of the latter forms are counted as two distinct readings.

[30]Ibid.

³¹Ibid., pp. 9-10.

³²P. R. McReynolds, "The Value and Limitations of the Claremont Profile Method" *Society of Biblical Literature 1972 Seminar Papers* (Missoula, Mont.: Society of Biblical Literature, 1972), p. 2.

³³Although the CPM initially makes tentative use of previously established text groups, independence is attained since the profiles carry their own criteria. See Wisse, "CPM," pp. 86-87.

³⁴McReynolds, "CPM," p. 6. The additional use of the CPM to organize large quantities of MSS is not relevant to the study of the text of the *PsSol*.

³⁵De la Cerda's edition cannot be considered to be a *textus receptus* since it has been identified by von Gebhardt as a poor copy of MS 149 and an unreliable witness to the text. See above, pp. 8-10.

³⁶A. Rahlfs, ed., *Septuaginta*, 7th edition, vol 2 (Stuttgart: Württembergische Bibelanstalt, 1935).

³⁷McReynolds, "CPM," p. 4. See p. 42 above.

³⁸Metzger, *Text*, pp. 189-192.

³⁹These readings are excluded only for the purposes of the CPM. A detailed examination of the characteristic readings of the MSS and text groups will appear in chapters four and five below.

⁴⁰These readings appear in the collation against the reading of the MSS and the designation "all witnesses."

⁴¹By confusion between the similar-sounding *alpha iota* and *epsilon*. See Metzger, *Text*, p. 190.

⁴²McReynolds, "CPM," p. 3; Wisse, "CPM," p. 90. Chapters 1, 10, and 20 were selected.

⁴³Block mixture is that phenomenon which occurs when a scribe changes from one exemplar to another in the process of his work. A copy may thus be produced of which different sections display different textual characteristics. See Colwell, *Studies in Methodology in Textual Criticism of the New Testament* (Grand Rapids: Eerdmans, 1969), pp. 66-70.

⁴⁴McReynolds, "CPM," p. 3; Wisse, "CPM," p. 90.

[45] Block mixtures up to several chapters in length could have been undetected if they had not appeared at the sample passages.

[46] The letters designate consecutively the variant readings in each verse. Thus, 1:1b is the omission of του by 253, 655, and 659 at that verse. Where readings have been combined, the letters appear together, as: 4:1ab. This system of designating the test readings is a departure from McReynolds and Wisse, who number the readings consecutively.

[47] Von Gebhardt, *Psalmen*, p. 39.

[48] McReynolds, "CPM," p. 20a.

[49] The significant variation is the word order.

[50] The significant variation is the word order.

[51] The significant variation is the presence or absence of the second του.

[52] McReynolds, "CPM," p. 9; Wisse, "CPM," p. 84.

[53] Wisse, "CPM," p. 85.

[54] Ibid., pp. 85-86; McReynolds, "CPM," p. 10.

[55] McReynolds, "CPM," p. 11. When, as is the case with the *PssSol*, there are only a few MS groups, one may expect a higher proportion of unique readings. When only 3 groups have been identified, any agreement between two is necessarily against a unique reading of the third.

[56] Omitting the corrected readings at 2:33b, 11:7g, and 15:4b.

[57] Omitting the corrected reading at 17:44a.

[58] The following are the number of readings by which the groups differ in each chapter: chapter 3-3; chapter 4-12; chapter 5-11; chapter 6-4; chapter 7-2; chapter 8-12; chapter 9-3; chapter 10-4; chapter 11-4; chapter 12-9; chapter 13-7; chapter 14-5; chapter 15-7.

[59] MSS 149, 260, 471, and 606 are identified by Joseph Ziegler as members of a text group for Wisdom and Sirach (*Sapientia Salomonis* [Gottingen: Vandenhoeck & Ruprecht, 1962], p. 48; *Sapientia Iesu Filii Sirach* [Göttingen: Vandenhoeck & Ruprecht, 1965], p. 56).

[60] McReynolds, "CPM," p. 11.

[61] Ibid., p. 20a.

[62] 2:5a, 4:18b, 6:4ab, 14:5b, 15:7b, and 17:30c.

[63] 3:10c, 4:18b, and 5:13b.

[64] 9:4a.

[65] 8:33c, 12:3f, 15:7f, and 15:13f.

[66] 4:8d, 5:5cd, 5:13c, 12:3c, 13:3a, 13:6f, and 14:5b. This does not include 5:1b, where 336 reads το ονομα with 471 and 606, since these are not a majority of the 260 group.

[67] Ziegler does not classify 336 as a member of any group for the text of Wisdom or Sirach (*Sapientia Salomonis*, pp. 60-61). The Sirach fragment which follows *PsSol* 18:4 is also without clear group affinities. See R. B. Wright and R. R. Hann, "A New Fragment of the Greek Text of Sirach" *JBL* 94:1 (1975) p. 112.

[68] McReynolds, "CPM," pp. 11-13; Wisse, "CPM," pp. 88-90.

[69] These readings represent peculiarities in the text of the 253 group. Agreements at these points cannot provide information about the relationship of 3004 to the other groups. To count these points would be to inflate artificially the degree of agreement between 3004 and the other MSS.

[70] Since 629 does not include the passage contained in 3004, the readings of 769 are taken to represent the 629-769 group.

[71] The exception is 17:3d, where an additional τον is read by 3004 and 769.

[72] In three of these instances, 471 is the only other member of the 260 group to have these readings: 17:25a, 17:29, and 18:9c. MSS 471 and 3004 are joined by 606 in reading ουδας at 17:21g.

NOTES TO CHAPTER FOUR

[1] McReynolds has written: "Variants that could be coincidental such as the omission of a pronoun can at times be considered as of less value than a transposition or an addition. Both of these facts must be kept in mind when one is classifying a new manuscript." P. R. McReynolds, "The Claremont Profile Method and the Grouping of Byzantine New Testament Manuscripts" (Ph.D. dissertation, Claremont Graduate School, 1968), p. 13.

[2] It will be recalled that the term "group" will be used of 336, although the latter is a single MS.

[3] See E. C. Colwell, *Studies in Methodology in Textual Criticism of the New Testament* (Grand Rapids: Eerdmans, 1969), pp. 57-60, where he discusses the effect of singular readings on calculations of MS relationships.

[4] The exception is the correction at 16:13.

[5] McReynolds, "CPM," p. 7.

[6] McReynolds uses these terms similarly in listing the characteristics of the test readings used in his application of the CPM: Ibid.

[7] Each of the characteristics which will be described with regard to MS 253 exceeds the requirement of occurring a total of two percent of the total number of readings.

[8] See Metzger, *Text*, p. 191.

[9] Cf. 8:26b, 13:7b, 13:9a, 13:10c, 14:1c, and 18:7b. Παιδεια is spelled παιδια by 253 at 7:9a and 16:13bc.

[10] This is not an uncommon exchange. See A. T. Robertson, *A Grammar of the Greek New Testament in the Light of Historical Research* (New York: Hodder & Stoughton, 1914), pp. 183-184. In 253 this exchange occurs at 2:2b, 2:11de, 2:13a, 3:6b, 4:16ce, 8:14a, 16:3a, 17:27c, 17:36, and 17:44d.

[11] Ibid., pp. 197-199. In 253 these occur at 3:5e, 6:4b, 10:1c, 15:12c, 16:2, and 17:28b.

[12] 6:4b, 16:2, and 17:28b.

[13] F. Blass and A. Debrunner, *A Greek Grammar of the New Testament and Other Early Christian Literature*, trans. and rev. by Robert W. Funk (Chicago: University of Chicago Press, 1961), p. 37.

Notes to pp. 57-60   131

[14] 2:31bc, 3:5c, 4:5d, 6:3f, 7:8ef, 8:8c, 8:11b, and 15:13a. See Metzger, *Text*, p. 190.

[15] 1:2c, 1:3a, 5:14d, 7:1b, 8:2a, 8:7c, 8:15b, 8:18b, 16:1d, and 16:3b.

[16] Robertson, *Grammar*, p. 220.

[17] 2:35a, 2:36b, 4:22a, 11:7a, and 17:23c.

[18] 5:5f, 6:4d, 8:2b, 11:5a, 17:40f, and 17:41a.

[19] 1:5a, 2:22g, 6:5a, 10:8a, 17:10c, 17:26, 17:30c, and 17:40a.

[20] 15:8b and 17:9a. See G. B. Gray, "The Psalms of Solomon," in *APOT* 2:648. The other examples are 4:19, 8:12g, 15:2e, 17:14a, 17:22e, and 17:32c.

[21] A nonsense reading is a reading produced by error, which does not make sense grammatically or contextually. See J. Finegan, *Encountering New Testament Manuscripts* (Grand Rapids: Eerdmans, 1974), p. 184. The errors which have resulted in nonsense readings can usually be explained, and the readings should be distinguished from meaningful forms which cannot be deciphered by present scholarship.

[22] The other instances are 1:4a, 5:3a, 5:9b, 8:7b, 8:9a, 8:20a, 9:1b, 9:5a, 14:3e, 16:8b, 17:30a, and 18:7b.

[23] The exceptions are 1:4a and 2:22f.

[24] 6:3c, 10:4b, 14:8a, 15:11b, and 18:3b.

[25] The other instances are 8:8b, 9:6d, 9:8d, 14:2e, 17:23e, 17:36c, 17:41g, and 18:4b.

[26] Since this is an obscure word, it has been misread by 655 and omitted altogether by 659.

[27] The other instances are 8:28e, 17:6a, and 17:6c.

[28] See Metzger, *Text*, p. 210.

[29] The use of paper began in the late middle ages. Its use in 655 and 659, however, is not conclusive evidence of dating, since the use of parchment continued after paper began to be used. Metzger, *Text*, p. 5.

[30] Robertson, *Grammar*, p. 220.

[31] In addition, the large number of readings shared by 655 and 659 reinforces the possibility that these were copied from a common exemplar.

[32] Scribes frequently introduced changes in the interest of improving the reading of the exemplar. Metzger, *Text*, pp. 209-210.

[33] Ibid.

[34] This passage is omitted by 629.

[35] O. von Gebhardt, *Die Psalmen Salomo's* (Leipzig: J. C. Hinrichs'sche Buchhandlung, 1895), p. 69. The difference in the final vowel, which von Gebhardt does not discuss, has resulted from itacism.

[36] Proportionately, if 3004 had contained the entire *PssSol* one might expect 93 variant readings in that witness. This is still fewer than the 237 variants in 253.

[37] παιδειαν is spelled πεδιαν in 253 and 659 and πεδιεαν in 655.

[38] The critical editions vary in their readings of the correction. Εν πευια παιδειαν is read as the uncorrected reading of 260 by Ryle and James, as the original reading of 149 and the corrected reading of 260 by Swete's 1894 edition, and as the original reading of 149 and 260 by Swete's 1899 edition. H. E. Ryle and M. R. James, *The Psalms of the Pharisees, Commonly Called the Psalms of Solomon* (Cambridge: University Press, 1891), p. 124; H. B. Swete, *The Old Testament in Greek According to the Septuagint* (Cambridge: University Press, 1894, 3:783; The Psalms of Solomon with the Greek Fragments of the Book of Enoch (Cambridge: University Press, 1899), p. 19.

[39] So also von Gebhardt, *Psalmen*, p. 23.

[40] Robertson, *Grammar*, p. 220.

[41] The spelling of αφαιρεθειη varies in 655 and 659.

[42] W. F. Arndt and F. W. Gignrich, eds., and trans., *Greek-English Lexicon of the New Testament and Other Early Christian Literature*. Eng. transl. of W. Bauer's *Griechisch-Deutsches Wörterbuch des Neuen Testaments und der übrigen urchristlichen Literatur* (Chicago: University of Chicago Press, 1957), p. 23.

[43] The accusative follows αινεω at 1 Chron 16:35, 29:13; 2 Chron 6:26; Ps 62:6, 68:31, 99:4, 112:1, 112:3, 114:2, 148:5, 148:13; Sir 17:10, 51:12; and Joel 2:26.

⁴⁴In Wis 17:18 the noun is δρομος, not δρυμος as in *PsSol* 11:5d. The scribe of the exemplar of 471-606, however, may have been influenced by the similarly appearing words. MSS 471 and 606 read δρομος at Wis 17:18.

⁴⁵See the listing by von Gebhardt in *Psalmen*, pp. 20-22. In addition to those which he lists, there are the following: 1:1a, 8:1a, 10:1a, 11:1a, 14:1a, 15:1a, and 16:1g. The readings at 8:10 and 16:5 in von Gebhardt's list are not examples, since they are omissions in the middle of words, although occurring at the beginning of a line. The instance at 9:6 should also be omitted, since this is the omission of an article.

⁴⁶This should not be read as an intentional change to a second person singular verb, since the translation would then be: "You reproached the gentiles of Jerusalem. . . ."

⁴⁷It is characteristic of 471 to omit material which is not part of the text itself, including the title to the *PsSol*, the superscriptions to the psalms, and the colophon which follows the *PsSol* in the other MSS. There is no title preceding the prologue to Sirach on 179v, nor preceding the body of that book on 180r. The title which precedes the prologue on 179v is a later addition in roman characters, and the title to the body of Sirach on 180r is a later marginal addition.

⁴⁸Arndt and Gingrich, *Lexicon*, p. 249; Blass and Debrunner, *Grammar*, p. 29. See R. W. Funk, *A Beginning-Intermediate Grammar of Hellenistic Greek* (Missoula, Mont: Society of Biblical Literature, 1973), 1:147-148.

⁴⁹Κακων at 12:4b would be an unlikely reading on intrinsic grounds since it would destroy the parallelism of the following lines.

⁵⁰See Metzger, *Text*, p. 210.

⁵¹As observed by W. Baars, "A New Fragment of the Greek Version of the Psalms of Solomon," *VT* 11 (1961) p. 441. There is a marginal reference to de la Cerda at 18:5: "Cerda interpretatur, regno."

⁵²The reading at 17:41h has been corrected by the original scribe and so has been retained.

⁵³The total number of verses in the *PsSol* is 5.14 times the number preserved in 3004. There are 14 readings at which 3004 differs from 471. If the entire text of the *PsSol* were preserved in 3004, we might expect a total of 72 variants between that MS and 471.

⁵⁴Metzger, *Text*, p. 190.

⁵⁵Ibid., p. 187.

⁵⁶This correction is written above the original letters and in the same hand. The corrections on the basis of de la Cerda appear in the margins or between the lines of text.

⁵⁷This change was perhaps influenced by Gen 1:14. See Arndt and Gingrich, *Lexicon*, p. 880.

⁵⁸Von Gebhardt, *Psalmen*, p. 39.

⁵⁹By means of observing the pattern of agreements among the MSS, ουδας at 17:21g can be identified as a reading of the ancestral text of 471-606-3004. The omission of διαψαλμα at 17:29 and 18:9c is derived from the common ancestor of 471 and 3004. The omission of the superscriptions of the individual psalms took place in 471 or an ancestor subsequent to the branching of the 3004 text.

⁶⁰Von Gebhardt, *Psalmen*, pp. 23-25.

⁶¹Since a direct copy of 149-260 is no longer extant, we cannot know whether or not it preserved the *alpha* and *beta* of 149 and 260. In the absence of such evidence for the descent of the text from 149-260 to 471-606-3004, it is better to state that this portion of the text cannot be reconstructed, than to engage in what would be, at best, an educated guess.

⁶²The closest extant representative of the ancestral text of the 253 group is MS 253. MS 260 or the nearly identical 149 is the ancestor of the remaining members of the 260 group. MS 336 is a distinctive text type found in no other witnesses.

⁶³A witness containing readings resembling those of other text groups may represent a text which has been corrected on the basis of other text types. In this case, such a similarity of readings would be due to conflation, and would not indicate an early stage in the transmission of the text. See Metzger, *Text*, p. 200.

⁶⁴The text of 629 is complete from 2:27 to 16:8. There are several points, however, where the text cannot be read. These are noted in the collation in chapter two above, and no comparisons involving these passages are made.

⁶⁵It is unlikely that this should be understood as an intentional change in case, since the preceding εν requires that the following noun be in the dative.

⁶⁶Von Gebhardt is usually extremely precise in noting corrections and other changes in the witnesses. See, for instance, his discussion of 16:13b: *Psalmen*, p. 23. It cannot be inferred on the basis of his silence about the obliteration in

769 at 13:2c, however, that the damage is recent: von Gebhardt used a collation for 769, which might not have noted all corrections to the text. *Psalmen*, p. 29.

[67] A cursive *pi* might easily have been read as a *sigma tau*. See B. A. van Groningen, *Short Manual of Greek Palaeography* (Leiden: A. W. Sijthoff's Uitgeversmaatschappij, 1940), p. 33.

[68] Von Gebhardt rejects the possibility that 769 could have been the exemplar for 629 on the ground of the dates of the two MSS. *Psalmen*, p. 37.

NOTES TO CHAPTER FIVE

[1] Since it is a single witness, 336 was omitted from consideration in the previous chapter. Term "group" includes 336, although the latter is a single MS.

[2] The common ancestor to MSS 655-659 is descended from the same archetype as 253. Where 253 and either 655 or 659 agree, therefore, this reading may be taken to represent their common archetype.

[3] This problem cannot be solved with assurance. Readings which can be identified as early or probable original readings, of course, can be taken to reflect the inherited text tradition of 336 as a MS. Other readings, however, cannot be distinguished, since a copyist may reproduce even a difficult error without change.

[4] These are read as itacism rather than as substantive verb changes since no unambiguous examples of change between the indicative and subjunctive appear in the 253 group readings. Itacism has also occurred at 1:3c, 2:7b, 2:17a, 2:19a, 2:26a, 2:31b, 3:6a, 3:12f, 5:8a, 5:10e, 7:8e, 7:9b, 8:13, 9:2a, 13:6a, 14:4c, 17:36c, 17:38b, 18:4b, and 18:10b.

[5] 2:15b, 2:19f, 2:35e, 3:3a, 3:5b, 3:5d, 6:4a, 6:4f, 6:5b, 8:1b, 8:15a, 8:15f, 8:18c, 8:21a, 8:23a, 10:2e, 10:7a, 12:3g, 13:1b, 14:1b, and 17:9d.

[6] It will be recalled that a textual characteristic must equal two percent of the total number of readings in a witness with more than one hundred variants. Since there are 221 variants involving the 253 group, four variations in the length of the *o*-vowel represent the minimum necessary, by rounding off, for consideration as a textual characteristic.

[7] The significant variation for the 253 group is the presence of the initial *sigma*.

[8] No spelling variations occur in the 253 group requiring an error in minuscule witnesses for explanation.

[9] For a thorough discussion, see H. St. J. Thackeray, *A Grammar of the Old Testament in Greek* (Cambridge: University Press, 1909), I:195, 209-212. See also F. Blass and A. Debrunner, *A Greek Grammar of the New Testament and Other Early Christian Literature*, trans. and rev. by R. W. Funk (Chicago, University of Chicago Press, 1961), pp. 41, 43, and A. T. Robertson, *A Grammar of the Greek New Testament in the Light of Historical Research* (New York: Hodder and Stoughton, 1914), pp. 337-339, 348.

[10] Robertson notes that aorist and imperfect forms are often indistinguishable: *Grammar*, p. 882.

[11] Other instances are at 2:3a, 2:13b, 8:11b, 8:12h, 13:3d, and 17:15a.

[12] The use of ειπα is Attic as well as Hellenistic: Blass and Debrunner, *Grammar*, p. 43.

[13] Other instances are at 2:21a, 8:16f, 8:25b, 9:7f, and 13:3a. Thackeray notes that these endings have fallen into disuse by the time of the NT: *Grammar*, p. 195.

[14] W. F. Arndt and F. W. Gingrich, eds. and transl., *Greek-English Lexicon of the New Testament and other Early Christian Literature*. Eng. transl. of W. Bauer's *Griechisch-Deutsches Wörterbuch zu den Schriften des Neuen Testaments und der übrigen urchristlichen Literatur* (Chicago: University of Chicago Press, 1957), p. 249. Thackeray, *Grammar*, p. 158. NT examples are Matt 9:13, 12:7, 23:23; Tit 3:5, and Heb 4:16.

[15] Arndt and Gingrich, *Lexicon*, p. 338; Thackeray, *Grammar*. p. 158. See also O. von Gebhardt, *Die Psalmen Salomo's* (Leipzig: J. C. Hinrichs'sche Buchhandlung, 1914), p. 31.

[16] Other instances are at 6:3a, 13:7c, and 18:12a. The case at 2:14 is doubtful, since the 253 group witnesses are not unanimous.

[17] Thackeray includes a quotation from a papyrus, but with an intervening article: *Grammar*, pp. 174-175.

[18] Other instances are at 3:3b, 3:4b, 3:12b, 4:23a, 8:19b, 10:2c, and 14:3c.

[19] Blass and Debrunner, *Grammar*, p. 184; Robertson, *Grammar*, p. 1174.

[20] There are no other instances of the addition of μη in the *PssSol*.

[21] 1:1b, 2:6a, 8:10a, 8:28d, 9:11a, 10:5b, 13:5, 14:5b, 15:10b, 17:7, 17:18a, and 18:6b.

[22] This may also have been the case at 9:9f where, however, εις is preceded by the ending -ει.

[23] 8:28d, 10:5b, 13:5c, 17:7, and 17:18a.

[24] 4:4a and 6:4h.

25The semitic noun with a pronominal suffix, the functional equivalent of the Greek genitive personal pronoun, does not take the article. R. A. Martin, *Syntactical Evidence of Semitic Sources in Greek Documents* (Cambridge, Massachusetts: The Society of Biblical Literature, 1974), p. 28.

26Other instances are at 4:20a, 5:5g, 5:14e, 13:6d, 15:7b, 15:13d, 17:3b, 17:15e, 17:43a, and 18:10a.

27Blass and Debrunner, *Grammar*, p. 35; Thackeray, *Grammar*, pp. 190-191.

28Arndt and Gingrich, *Lexicon*, p. 811; Blass and Debrunner, *Grammar*, p. 17; Thackeray, *Grammar*, p. 63.

29Other substitutions occur at 2:11f, 2:13c, 2:31d, 4:1d, 4:8g, 5:11bc, 9:3d, 9:5b, 15:1d, and 17:33d.

30Εξουθενοω occurs only four times in Alexandrinus, Sinaiticus, and Vaticanus: Thackeray, *Grammar*, p. 105.

31Ibid., pp. 222-223. There are only three exceptions in the uncials.

32Arndt and Gingrich, *Lexicon*, p. 775; Blass and Debrunner, *Grammar*, p. 39.

33B. M. Metzger, *The Text of the New Testament* (New York: Oxford University Press, 1968), p. 187.

34Ibid.

35J. H. Moulton and G. Milligan, *The Vocabulary of the Greek New Testament* (Grand Rapids, Michigan: Eerdmans, 1952), p. 226.

36The genitive singular of the 253 group and 769 is read by 336 as the genitive plural.

37Metzger, *Text*, p. 187.

38Γαρ does not precede μαρτυρια in the following line of 10:4 in the 260 group.

39The regular use of εν in place of other prepositions is a characteristic of translation Greek: Martin, *Evidence*, pp. 5-15.

40Απολουνται does not fit the context and could not have been the original reading. The addition of the *sigma* to αμαρτωλου and the resultant change in case is required by the verb change, and may have been a subsequent change within the 260 group tradition.

[41] So J. Viteau, *Les Psaumes de Salomon* (Paris: Letouzey et Ané, 1911), p. 332. Viteau, however, prints both lines, and concludes that the line at 15:12cd was omitted be homoeoteleuton. Von Gebhardt (*Psalmen*, p. 46) follows the non-260 reading on the basis of the spelling error in the 260 group. In addition, an assertion that the transposition is a conscious rearrangement by the 260 group fails, since no other intentional rearrangement exists in this text group.

[42] The reading at 12:3b is understood as an itacism rather than as a change in declension, since there are no clear instances of such change in 336. On the other hand, the readings at 5:5d and 5:6a are classified as changes in mood rather than as itacism, since other examples of change in mood can be found in this MS.

[43] Thackeray, *Grammar*, pp. 138-139. This distinction is not observed in the NT: Arndt and Gingrich, *Lexicon*, p. 81.

[44] Metzger, *Text*, p. 187.

[45] Επι may have its object in either the genitive or the accusative. Υετον επι της γης and υετον επι την γην are found in the LXX in approximately equal numbers.

[46] The MSS vary with regard to the final *nu*, added by the 253 group. Other examples of exchange between the future indicative and aorist subjunctive are 5:5d and 9:9c. These are not discussed above, since the non-336 witnesses are not agreed.

[47] Blass and Debrunner, *Grammar*, p. 183; R. Browning, *Medieval and Modern Greek* (London: Hutchinson University Library, 1969), p. 41.

[48] Reading as an infinitive rather than as an optative, since the latter becomes rare in Koine Greek: R. Browning, *Greek*, p. 41.

[49] Οταν and μη both take the subjunctive: Arndt and Gingrich, *Lexicon*, pp. 592, 513. The use of the indicative is due to the phonetic similarity between the two forms: Browning, *Greek*, p. 37.

[50] Martin, *Evidence*, p. 28.

[51] Metzger, *Text*, pp. 189-190.

[52] Ibid., pp. 203-206.

[53]Ενυξεν, for example, (16:4a) occurs in the LXX only twice: Sir 22:19 and 3 Macc 5:14.

[54]Jud 7:19, 1 Esd 5:59, Ps 139:2, Matt 22:53.

[55]Cf. Matt 14:12, Mark 15:45; see Arndt and Gingrich, *Lexicon*, p. 735.

[56]Cf. the reading πομα for πνευμα at 1 Cor 12:13, described by Metzger (*Text*, p. 187). The parallels at Isa 1:4 and 14:20 are not sufficiently similar for dependence.

[57]MS 336 reads απαρχης.

[58]There is thereby produced a change in orientation. The divine judgment is expected not on the events of the first two verses, but on τη καρδια μου.

[59]With the omission of the article at 15:13d, the reading of the 629 group resembles that of 336.

[60]It will be noted that the combinations: 253 + 260 against 336 + 629; 253 + 336 against 260 + 269; and 253 + 629 against 260 + 336 represent all possible combinations in pairs of the four groups.

[61]This passage is omitted in 629.

[62]This passage is omitted in 629.

[63]Thackeray, *Grammar*, p. 115; Browning, *Greek*, pp. 33-34.

[64]Metzger, *Text*, p. 190.

[65]This passage is omitted in 629.

[66]The word is preceded by εν in Zech 3:2.

[67]Browning, *Greek*, pp. 42-43. The dative case finally passed out of use: p. 64.

[68]2:22, 23; 4:4, 15, 25; 5:1, 11, 15; 8:31, 33; 9:3, 9; 12:1; 17:1, 4, 21; 18:1.

[69]Blass and Debrunner, *Grammar*, p. 81; Robertson, *Grammar*, pp. 462-463. The vocative is used in the papyri: Robertson, pp. 365-366.

[70]The reading of MS 253, εισωφροσυνην, is an error. MSS 655-659 have reproduced the group reading correctly.

Notes to pp. 88-92   141

[71] Esth 3:13; Wis 8:7; 2 Macc 4:37; 4 Macc 1:3, 6, 18, 30, 31, 5:23. None of these occurs in a similar context.

[72] See above, p. 98.

[73] Metzger, *Text*, p. 190.

[74] Thackeray, *Grammar*, pp. 214-215; Blass and Debrunner, *Grammar*, pp. 44-45.

[75] Ps 85:12; 110:1; 118:2, 10, 34, 55, 69, 145; 137:1.

[76] Job 36:30 and Zech 4:7.

[77] Metzger, *Text*, p. 187.

[78] Cf. also Jdt 16:13 and Isa 42:10.

[79] Thackeray, *Grammar*, pp. 138-139.

[80] This list of characteristics is from P. R. McReynolds, "The Claremont Profile Method and the Grouping of Byzantine New Testament Manuscripts" (Ph.D. dissertation, Claremont Graduate School, 1968), p. 7.

NOTES TO CHAPTER SIX

[1] B. F. Westcott and F. J. Hort, *The New Testament in the Original Greek* Cambridge: Macmillan, 1882), p. 40.

[2] O. von Gebhardt, *Die Psalmen Salomo's* (Leipzig: J. C. Hinrichs'sche Buchhandlung, 1985), pp. 30-32.

[3] Von Gebhardt, *Psalmen*, p. 34. Of special interest for von Gebhardt is the shared reading at 4:8e.

[4] 3:12b, 4:8a, 3:2c, 17:41c.

[5] Von Gebhardt, *Psalmen*, pp. 38-39.

[6] B. M. Metzger, *The Text of the New Testament* (New York: Oxford University Press, 1968), p. 157: "...apart from accident, identity of reading implies identity of origin."

[7] H. St. J. Thackeray, *A Grammar of the Old Testament in Greek* (Cambridge: University Press, 1909), I:138-139. The NT varies: see W. F. Arndt and F. W. Gingrich, eds. and transl., *Greek-English Lexicon of the New Testament and Other Early Christian Literature*. Eng. transl. of W. Bauer's *Griechisch-Deutsches Wörterbuch zu den Schriften des Neuen Testaments und der übrigen urchristlichen Literatur*. (Chicago: University of Chicago Press, 1957), p. 81; F. Blass and A. Debrunner, *A Greek Grammar of the New Testament and Other Early Christian Literature*, trans. and rev. by R. W. Funk (Chicago: University of Chicago Press, 1961), p. 143.

[8] This reading is found in 336 alone at 9:6i; see above.

[9] The alternative, that 260-336 are original and 253 -629 the variations, presents the same difficulties.

[10] S. Jellicoe, *The Septuagint and Modern Study* (Oxford: Clarendon Press, 1968), p. 348.

[11] Metzger, *Text*, p. 159.

[12] The relatively small number of readings shared between the 260 and 629 groups against the 253 group and 336 is due to the care of the copyist of *t*.

[13] This is the sum of all probable original readings in 260 and readings where the 253 group agrees with either the 260 or 629 groups.

Notes to pp. 103-108

[14] It cannot be determined whether the remaining witnesses of the 260 group are copied from 149 or 260.

[15] R. Curzon, *Visits to Monasteries in the Levant* (London: Arthur Barker Ltd., 1955), pp. 307, 298.

[16] P. Charanis, "The Monastic Properties and State in the Byzantine Empire", *Dumbarton Oaks Papers, 1948* (Cambridge: Harvard University Press, 1948), p. 94; E. A. de Mendietta, *Mount Athos* (Berlin: Akademie-Verlag, 1972), p. 87.

[17] Ibid., p. 248. Among the MSS removed from Mt. Athos was 471 and the remainder of the five hundred MSS which Sukharov brought to Moscow in 1654.

[18] Lambros was not permitted to examine the MSS of the Laura monastery carefully. (Ibid., p. 224) Catalogs of the MSS of Vatopedi and of Laura were published in 1924 and 1925, respectively. (Ibid., p. 244)

[19] This follows Westcott and Hort's statement that one should utilize the "best documentary representatives" of the lines of transmission: *New Testament*, p. 59.

[20] If any probable original readings had been found among the readings of these MSS against 149-260, an assumption of textual mixture would have been required. This, however, is not the case.

[21] Westcott and Hort, *New Testament*, p. 31: "Knowledge of documents should precede final judgement upon readings."

[22] See Metzger's catalog of common scribal errors (*Text*, pp. 187-192). Exceptions are where a spelling change has produced a grammatical or lexical variation that suits the context. This has occurred in the *PsSol* at 15:7e and 17:31a.

[23] Thackeray, *Grammar*, p. 71. See P. Walters, *The Text of the Septuagint* (Cambridge: University Press, 1973), in which he challenges some of the spellings adopted by the Cambridge and Göttingen editions of the LXX.

[24] See Westcoot and Hort, *New Testament*, p. 1.

[25] Metzger, *Text*, p. 210.

[26] Ibid., pp. 189-190.

[27] Singular readings are, by the usual canons, to be treated with caution in any event. (See Westcott and Hort, *New Testament*, p. 44.) This principle is less useful, however, when dealing with a writing of which only 11 MSS exist.

[28] It is not possible to quantify the relative proportions of probable original readings into a statement of mathematical probability, since the nature of these readings varies. Thirty-nine of the probable original readings in MS 253 are repetitions of two characteristics.

[29] The 260 group can follow its own recension only by departing from the ancestor which it shares with the 629 group.

[30] There can be an exception only if the original reading has been preserved by none of the extant witnesses.

[31] The 629 group readings must recapitulate either the 253 or the 336 text tradition, or have originated by a subsequent error.

[32] With the exception of the 629 group, whose singular readings are always incorrect, the 260 group preserves probable original readings least frequently. See above, pp. 105-109.

[33] Westcott and Hort, *New Testament*, p. 21.

[34] Metzger, *Text*, pp. 197-198.

[35] Ibid., p. 210.

[36] Ibid., pp. 209-210.

[37] Westcott and Hort, *New Testament*, p. 22.

[38] So also Metzger, *Text*, p. 209.

[39] For a cross-cultural study of the textual criticism of non-biblical materials, see Metzger's article, "Trends in the Textual Criticism of the Iliad and the Mahabharata," *Chapters in the History of New Testament Textual Criticism* (Grand Rapids: Eerdmans, 1963), pp. 142-154.

[40] "Genealogical presumptions. . . ought to take precedence. . . because their immediate basis is historical and not speculative." Westcott and Hort, *New Testament*, p. 63.

[41] There can be an exception only if the subsequent scribe has coincidentally produced the same reading as the original author. See Westcott and Hort, ibid., p. 69. A reading is to be considered conjectural even if attested in the MSS if it has not been transmitted from the autographs.

[42] Examples are the dittography at 1:4d and the use of the final *nu* at 8:2a and 8:7c.

Notes to pp. 113-114

[43] Cf. Jellicoe, *Septuagint*, pp. 305-310.

[44] J. Ziegler, *Sapientia Salomonis* (Göttingen: Vandenhoeck & Ruprecht, 1962), pp. 50-53; *Sapientia Iesu Filii Sirach* (Göttengen: Vandenhoeck & Ruprecht, 1965). pp. 57-63.

[45] Ziegler, *Sapientia Salomonis*, pp. 48, 61; *Sirach*, pp. 56, 70.

[46] Cf. the following articles by Ziegler: "Hat Lukian den griechischen Sirach rezensiert?" *Biblica* (40) 1959, pp. 210-229; "Die hexaplaeische Bearbeitung des griechischen Sirach," *Biblische Zeitschrift* (N.F. 4) 1960, pp. 174-185; "Die Vokabel-Varianten der O-Rezension im griechischen Sirach," in *Hebrew and Semitic Studies Presented to Godfrey Rolles Driver*, ed. by D. W. Thomas and W. D. McHardy (Oxford: Clarendon Press, 1963), pp. 172-180.

[47] Jellicoe, *Septuagint*, p. 125.

[48] J. Begrich, "Der Text der Psalmen Salomos" *ZNW* 38 (1939), p. 154.

[49] Jellicoe, *Septuagint*, pp. 100-106.

[50] To the present writer's knowledge, the present work is the first application of the CPM to materials of the pseudepigrapha. Other writings of the pseudepigrapha extant in only a few witnesses are The Letter of Aristeas, Sybilline Oracles, Testaments of the Twelve Patriarchs, and the Assumption of Moses. See the descriptions of these in A. M. Denis, *Introduction aux Pseudepigraphes grecs d'Ancien Testament* (Leiden: Brill, 1970) and L. Rost, *Einleitung in die alttestamentlichen Apokryphen und Pseudepigraphen* (Heidelberg: Quelle & Meyer, 1971). According to Rost, the most recent full-scale textual studies of the Letter of Aristeas and of the Assumption of Moses were in 1714 and 1904, respectively.

[51] The Society of Biblical Literature's Pseudepigrapha Series is not intended to meet this need: "No effort is made in these publications to provide new critical texts, nor to furnish extensive annotations. The series is regarded as provisional, and individual volumes may be replaced in the future when better textual evidence is available." *Paraleipomena Jeremiou*, ed. and transl. by R. A. Kraft and A. E. Purintun (Missoula, Mont.: Society of Biblical Literature, 1972), p. i.

BIBLIOGRAPHY

Articles

Baars, W. "A New Fragment of the Greek Version of the Psalms of Solomon." *VT* 11 (1961): 441-444.

Begrich, Joachim. "Der Text der Psalmen Salomos." *ZNW* 18 (1939): 131-164.

Charanis, Peter. "The Monastic Properties and State in the Byzantine Empire." In *Dumbarton Oaks Papers, 1948.* Cambridge: Harvard University Press, 1948.

Colwell, Ernest C. "External Evidence and New Testament Criticism." In *Studies in the History and Text of the New Testament*, ed. by Boyd L. Daniels and M. Jack Suggs. Salt Lake City: University of Utah Press, 1967.

_____. "The Greek New Testament With a Limited Textual Apparatus: Its Nature and Uses." In *Studies in the New Testament and Early Christian Literature*, ed. by David Edward Aune. Leiden: Brill, 1972.

_____. "The International Greek New Testament Project: a Status Report." *JBL* 87 (1968): 187-197.

Epp, Eldon Jay. "The Claremont Profile-Method for Grouping New Testament Minuscule Manuscripts." In *Studies in the History and Text of the New Testament*, ed. by Boyd L. Daniels and M. Jack Suggs. Salt Lake City: University of Utah Press, 1967.

Gray, G. Buchanan. "The Psalms of Solomon." In R. H. Charles' *APOT*. Oxford: Clarendon Press, 1913, 2:625-652.

Harris, J. Rendel. "Notes on the Sinaitic and Vatican Codices." *Johns Hopkins University Circular* 29 (March, 1884): 54.

Hilgenfeld, A. "Die Himmelfahrt des Moses." *ZWT* 11 (1868): 133-168.

McReynolds, Paul R. "The Value and Limitations of the Claremont Profile Method." *Society of Biblical Literature 1972 Seminar Papers*. Missoula, Mont.: Society of Biblical Literature, 1972.

Metzger, Bruce M. "Recent Developments in the Textual Criticism of the New Testament." In his *Historical and Literary Studies*. Leiden: Brill, 1968.

_____. "Trends in the Textual Criticism of the Iliad and the the Mahābhārata. In his *Chapters in the History of New Testament Textual Criticism*. Grand Rapids: Eerdmans, 1963.

Pesch, Wilhelm. "Die Abhangigkeit des 11. salomonischen Psalms vom Letzten Kapitel des Buches Baruch." *ZAW* 67 (1955): 251-263.

Pick, Bernard. "The Psalter of Solomon." *Presbyterian Review*, 1883, pp. 775-812.

Wright, Robert. "The Psalms of Solomon, the Pharisees, and the Essenes." International Organization for Septuagintal and Cognate Studies, *1972 Proceedings*. Missoula, Mont.: Scholars Press, 1972.

Wright, Robert B., and Hann, Robert R. "A New Fragment of the Greek Text of Sirach." *JBL* 94 (1975): 111-112.

Ziegler, Joseph. "Die hexaplarische Bearbeitung des griechischen Sirach." *BZ* N.F. 4 (1960): 174-185.

_____. "Hat Lukian den griechischen Sirach rezensiert?" *Biblica* 40 (1959): 219-229.

_____. "Die Vokabel-Varianten der O-Rezension im griechischen Sirach." In *Hebrew and Semitic Studies Presented to Godfrey Rolles Driver*, ed. by D. Winton Thomas and W. D. McHardy. Oxford: Clarendon Press, 1963.

Books

Arndt, William F., and Gingrich, F. Wilbur, eds. and transl. *Greek-English Lexicon of the New Testament and Other Early Christian Literature*. Eng. tr. of Walter Bauer's *Griechisch-Deutsches Wörterbuch des Neuen Testaments und der übrigen urchristlichen Literatur*. Chicago: University of Chicago Press, 1961.

Baars, W. *Psalms of Solomon*. Leiden: Brill, 1972.

Blass, F., and Debrunner, A. *A Greek Grammar of the New Testament and Other Early Christian Literature*, trans. and rev. by Robert W. Funk. Chicago: University of Chicago Press, 1961.

Browning, Robert. *Medieval and Modern Greek*. London: Hutchinson University Library, 1969.

Codex Alexandrinus. London: British Museum, 1915.

Colwell, Ernest C. *Studies in Methodology in Textual Criticism of the New Testament*. Grand Rapids: Eerdmans, 1969.

Curzon, Robert. *Visits to Monasteries in the Levant*. London: Arthur Barker Ltd., 1955.

de Jonge, M. *De Toekomstverwachting in de Psalmen van Salomo*. Leiden: Brill, 1965.

de la Cerda, Juan Luis. *Adversaria Sacra*. Lyon: n. p., 1626.

de Mendietta, Emmanuel Amand. *Mount Athos*. Berlin: Akademie-Verlag, 1972.

Denis, Albert-Marie. *Introduction aux Pseudépigraphes grecs d'Ancien Testament.* Leiden: Brill, 1970.

Dupont-Sommer, A. *The Essene Writings of Qumran.* Cleveland: Meridian, 1966.

Fabricius, J. A. *Codex pseudepigraphus Veteris Testamenti.* Hamburg and Leipzig: n.p., 1713.

Finegan, Jack. *Encountering New Testament Manuscripts.* Grand Rapids: Eerdmans, 1974.

Frankenberg, Wilhelm. *Die Datierung der Psalmen Salomos.* Giessen: J. Ricker'sche Buchhandlung, 1896.

Fritzsche, Otto Fridolinus. *Libri apocryphi Veteris Testamenti pseudepigraphi selecti.* Leipzig: F.A. Brockhaus, 1871.

Funk, Robert W. *A Beginning-Intermediate Grammar of Hellenistic Greek.* Missoula, Mont.: Society of Biblical Literature, 1973.

Gates, John Edward. *An Analysis of Lexicographic Resources Used by American Biblical Scholars Today.* Missoula, Mont.: Society of Biblical Literature, 1972.

Geiger, E. E. *Der Psalter Salomo's herausgegeben und erklärt.* Augsburg: n.p., 1871.

Harris, J. Rendel. *The Odes and Psalms of Solomon.* Cambridge: University Press, 1909.

Harris, J. Rendel, and Mingana, Alphonse. *The Odes and Psalms of Solomon.* Manchester: University Press, 1916.

Hilgenfeld, Adolphus. *Messias Judaeorum.* Leipzig: Fuesianus, 1869.

Jellicoe, Sidney. *The Septuagint and Modern Study.* Oxford: Clarendon Press, 1968.

Kuhn, K. G. *Die älteste Textgestalt der Psalmen Salomos.* Stuttgart: W. Kohlhammer Verlag, 1937.

McReynolds, Paul R. "The Claremont Profile Method and the Grouping of Byzantine New Testament Manuscripts." Ph.D. dissertation, Claremont Graduate School, 1969.

Martin, Raymond A. *Syntactical Evidence of Semitic Sources in Greek Documents.* Cambridge, Mass.: Society of Biblical Literature, 1974.

Metzger, Bruce M. *Annotated Bibliography of the Textual Criticism of the New Testament 1914-1939.* Copenhagen: Ejnar Munksgaard, 1955.

_____. *The Text of the New Testament.* New York: Oxford University Press, 1968.

Bibliography

Moulton, James Hope, and Milligan, George. *The Vocabulary of the Greek New Testament*. Grand Rapids: Eerdmans, 1952.

Neusner, Jacob. *From Politics to Piety, the Emergence of Pharisaic Judaism*. Englewood Cliffs, N.J.: Prentice-Hall, 1973.

Nestle, Eberhard, Nestle, Erwin, and Aland, Kurt, eds. *Novum Testamentum Graece*, 25th ed. Stuttgart: Württembergische Bibelanstalt, 1935.

Rahlfs, Alfred, ed. *Septuaginta*, 7th ed., vol. 2. Stuttgart: Württembergische Bibelanstalt, 1927.

_____. *Verzeichnis der griechischen Handschriften des Alten Testaments*. Göttingen: K. Gesellschaft der Wissenschaften, 1914.

Robertson, A. T. *A Grammar of the Greek New Testatent in the Light of Historical Research*. New York: Hodder and Stoughton, 1914.

Rost, Leonhard. *Einleitung in die alttestamentlichen Apokryphen und Pseudepigraphen*. Heidelberg: Quelle & Meyer, 1971.

Ryle, Herbert Edward, and James, Montague Rhodes. *The Psalms of the Pharisees, commonly called the Psalms of Solomon*. Cambridge: University Press, 1981.

Sandmel, Samuel. *The First Christian Century in Judaism and Christianity*. New York: Oxford University Press, 1969.

Schüpphaus, Joachim. *Die Psalmen Salomos*. Leiden: Brill, 1977.

Swete, Henry Barclay. *The Old Testament in Greek according to the Septuagint*, vol. 3. Cambridge: University Press, 1894.

_____. *The Psalms of Solomon with the Greek Fragments of the Book of Enoch*. Cambridge: University Press, 1899.

Thackeray, Henry St. John. *A Grammar of the Old Testament in Greek*, vol. 1. Cambridge: University Press, 1909.

Viteau, J. *Les Psaumes de Salomon*. Paris: Letouzey et Ané, 1911.

van Groningen, B. A. *A Short Manual of Greek Paleography*. Leiden: A. W. Sijthoff's Uitgeversmaatschappij, 1940.

von Gebhardt, Oscar. *Die Psalmen Salomo's*. Leipzig: J. C. Hinrichs'sche Buchhandlung, 1895.

Walters, Peter. *The Text of the Septuagint*. Cambridge: University Press, 1973.

Wellhausen, Julius. *Die Pharisäer und die Sadducäer.*
Griefswald: np.p. 1874.

Westcott, Brooke Foss, and Hort, Fenton John Anthony. *The New Testament in the Original Greek.* Cambridge: Macmillan, 1882.

Wisse, Frederik. "The Claremont Profile Method for the Classification of Byzantine New Testament Manuscripts: a Study in Method." Ph.D. dissertation, Claremont Graduate School, 1968.

Wright, Robert. "The Psalms of Solomon: a Provisional Collated Greek Text." Philadelphia: Temple University, 1976.

Zahn, Theodor. *Geschichte des neutestamentlichen Kanons*, vol. 2. Erlangen: A. Deichert'sche Verlagsbuchhandlung, 1890.

Ziegler, Joseph. *Sapientia Iesu Filii Sirach.* Göttingen: Vandenhoeck & Ruprecht, 1965.

_____. *Sapientia Salomonis.* Göttingen: Vandenhoeck & Ruprecht, 1962.

INDEX TO PASSAGES

A. *PSALMS OF SOLOMON*

PsSol	1:	1	39, 128n46, 133n45, 137n21
		2	131n15
		3	89, 100, 131n15, 136n4
		4	61, 62, 63, 131n22, 131n23, 144n42
		5	69, 87, 99, 131n19
	2:	1	39
		2	77, 115n4, 130n10
		3	137n11
		4	82
		5	79, 81, 115n4
		6	78, 137n21
		7	136n4
		8	39, 77, 83, 89, 99
		9	87, 99
		11	38, 39, 57, 66, 79, 130n10, 138n29
		13	79, 92, 130n10, 137n11, 138n29
		14	87,99
		15	136n5
		17	39, 136n4
		19	39, 65, 82, 83, 136n4, 136n5
		21	39, 76, 87, 99, 137n13
		22	58, 61, 62, 64, 78, 79, 84, 85, 88, 131n19, 131n23, 140n68
		23	39, 65, 76, 79, 87, 140n68
		24	38, 76, 77, 83
		25	39, 78, 85, 111
		26	84, 136n4
		27	5, 81, 134n64
		29	66, 76, 88
		31	71, 90, 99, 131n14, 136n4, 138n29
		32	38, 71, 78, 111
		33	87
		35	71, 84, 130n11, 131n17
		36	71, 72, 73, 82, 88, 131n17
	3:	1	89,99
		2	85, 89, 142n4
		3	136n5, 137n18
		4	76, 79, 92, 137n18
		5	38, 66, 131n14, 136n5
		6	130n10, 136n4
		8	78, 86, 88
		9	84
		10	79, 85, 111
		11	38, 78, 83, 111
		12	78, 82, 89, 111, 136n4, 137n18, 142n3
	4:	1	39, 71, 79, 81, 84, 128n46, 138n29
		2	86
		3	77, 78
		4	59, 137n24, 140n68
		5	38, 131n14
		7	89
		8	72, 76, 77, 84, 88, 90, 99, 138n29, 142n3

151

PsSol 4: 9 81, 83, 88
        10 78, 81, 89, 99
        11 81
        12 38
        13 71, 81, 84
        15 59, 65, 78, 80, 81, 85, 111, 140n68
        16 57, 78, 111, 130n10
        17 71, 78
        19 131n20
        20 77, 86, 138n26
        21 39, 58, 62, 72, 77, 90, 100
        22 82, 131n17
        23 57, 137n18
     5: 1 38, 65, 68, 69, 140n68
        2 38, 59, 76, 77, 79
        3 81, 85, 86, 131n22
        4 80, 84, 130n11
        5 60, 62, 131n18, 138n26, 139n42, 139n46
        6 83, 139n42
        7 64
        8 83, 88, 136n4
        9 71, 72, 131n22
        10 88, 136n4
        11 71, 76, 81, 111, 138n29, 140n68
        12 77
        13 80, 90
        14 4, 131n15, 138n26
        16 81
     6: 3 89, 131n14, 131n24, 137n16
        4 39, 57, 64, 80, 130n12, 131n18, 136n5, 137n24
        5 131n19, 136n5
        6 66
     7: 1 131n15
        2 71
        7 86
        8 71, 131n14, 136n4
        9 130n9, 136n4
     8: 1 39, 71, 72, 73, 133n45, 136n5
        2 57, 86, 131n15, 131n18, 144n42
        3 86
        4 81
        5 4
        6 38, 39
        7 57, 131n15, 131n22, 144n42
        8 38, 39, 86, 131n14, 131n25
        9 71, 131n22
        10 65, 71, 133n45, 137n21
        11 131n14, 137n11
        12 4, 39, 65, 72, 77, 131n20, 137n11
        13 136n4
        14 80
        15 71, 84, 88, 130n10, 131n15, 136n5
        16 137n13
        17 82
        18 131n15, 136n5
        19 58, 60, 61, 63, 137n18
        20 63, 78, 131n22
        21 71, 136n5
        22 39, 71, 77

Passages   153

PsSol   8: 23   59, 136n5
             24   84
             25   137n13
             26   130n9
             28   66, 77, 131n27, 137n21, 137n23
             29   59
             30   59
             31   76, 77, 140n68
             33   59, 84, 86, 87, 88, 99, 140n68
             34   81, 83, 93, 99, 102
         9:   1   63, 65, 85, 131n22
              2   38, 81, 84, 136n4
              3   71, 138n29, 140n68
              4   89
              5   79, 81, 92, 131n22, 138n29
              6   65, 82, 85, 86, 90, 94, 111, 131n25, 133n45,
                  142n8
             ·7   39, 58, 71, 111, 137n13
              8   39, 60, 62, 83, 131n25
              9   137n22, 139n46, 140n68
             10   39
             11   59, 71, 137n21
        10:   1   82, 130n11, 133n45
              2   59, 86, 136n5, 137n18
              3   38, 39, 59
              4   81, 131n24, 138n38
              5   65, 84, 137n21, 137n23
              7   83, 136n5
              8   88, 100, 110, 131n19
        11:   1   59, 80, 83, 111, 133n45
              2   84
              4   77
              5   59, 68, 69, 71, 72, 133n44
              6   60
              7   79, 71, 72, 82, 86, 131n17
              8   81, 111
        12:   1   71, 72, 73, 140n68
              2   66, 71, 81, 82
              3   71, 82, 83, 136n5, 139n42
              4   66, 82, 133n49
              5   78
              6   72, 83
        13:   1   71, 136n5
              2   72
              3   59, 72, 84, 137n11, 137n13
              4   71, 100
              5   137n23
              6   65, 69, 86, 90, 136n4, 137n21, 138n26
              7   86, 130n9, 137n16
              8   82
              9   76, 130n9
             10   59, 82, 130n9
             11   82
        14:   1   130n9, 133n45, 136n5
              2   78, 83, 131n25,
              3   58, 111, 131n22, 137n18
              4   82, 136n4
              5   59, 61, 62, 81, 90, 111, 137n21
              7   71, 72, 73, 81

PsSol 14: 8   79, 86, 92, 131n24
         9   59, 77
        10   71
    15: 1   84, 133n45, 138n29
         2   59, 81, 82, 84, 131n20
         3   80, 83, 86, 89
         4   86
         5   38
         7   83, 86, 100, 138n26, 143n22
         8   39, 59, 62, 71, 77, 87, 111, 131n20
         9   82
        10   76, 84, 94, 137n21
        11   82, 131n24
        12   81, 93, 99, 102, 111, 130n11, 139n41
        13   86, 131n14, 138n26, 140n59
    16: 1   66, 82, 84, 85, 131n15, 133n45
         2   130n11, 130n12
         3   84, 85, 131n15
         4   71, 140n53
         5   39, 72, 73, 82, 130n10, 133n45
         7   84
         8   5, 88, 131n22
         9   82
        11   82
        12   60, 66, 79
        13   9, 63, 64, 69, 81, 130n9
    17: 1   84, 140n68
         2   6, 10, 68
         3   67, 70, 77, 83, 138n26
         4   59, 87, 140n68
         5   59, 65, 82, 84, 85, 137n11
         6   67, 80, 82, 131n27
         7   137n21, 137n23
         8   65
         9   81, 89, 99, 131n20, 136n5
        10   83, 131n19
        11   38, 59, 60, 62, 67, 70, 80, 82, 85
        12   6, 39, 67, 83
        13   58, 65, 84
        14   131n20
        15   58, 82
        16   77
        17   115n5
        18   82, 83, 137n21, 137n23
        19   67, 70
        20   1, 83
        21   1, 64, 67, 69, 84, 134n59, 140n68
        22   67, 70, 131n20
        23   65, 80, 85, 131n17, 131n25
        24   84
        25   65, 67, 70
        26   131n19
        27   57, 67, 70, 79, 130n10
        28   130n11, 130n12
        29   65, 67, 134n59
        30   67, 78, 111, 131n19, 131n22
        31   59, 87, 143n22
        32   67, 85, 131n20
        33   59, 67, 138n29

Passages

PsSol	17:	35	66, 89
		36	76, 88, 130n10, 131n25, 136n4
		37	84
		38	76, 88, 136n4
		39	66
		40	60, 83, 131n18, 131n19
		41	66, 67, 89, 111, 131n18, 131n25, 133n52, 142n4
		42	85
	43	43	80, 84, 138n26
		44	81, 85, 130n10
		45	39
	18:	1	79, 140n68
		3	77, 131n24
		4	81, 82, 131n25, 136n4
		5	11, 67
		6	137n21
		7	130n9, 131n22
		8	81
		9	65, 77, 87, 99, 115n1, 134n59
		10	67, 70, 136n4, 138n26
		12	137n16

B. OLD TESTAMENT AND APOCRYPHA

Gen	1:	14	134n57
Judg	7:	19	140n54
1 Chr	16:	35	132n43
	29:	13	132n43
2 Chr	6:	26	132n43
1 Esdr	5:	59	140n54
Esth	3:	13	141n71
Jdt	16:	13	141n78
Tob	13:	2	85
	14:	9	85
2 Macc	4:	37	141n71
3 Macc	5:	14	140n53
4 Macc	1:	3	141n71
		6	141n71
		18	141n71
		30	141n71
		31	141n71
	5:	23	141n71
Ps	39:	4	89
	62:	6	132n43
	68:	31	132n43
	85:	12	141n75
	99:	4	132n43
	104:	14	81
	110:	1	141n75
	112:	1	132n43
	112:	3	132n43
	114:	2	132n43
	118:	2	141n75
		10	141n75
		34	141n75
		55	141n75
		69	141n75
		145	141n75

Ps	137:	1	141n75
	139:	2	140n54
	148:	5	132n43
		13	132n43
Job	36:	30	141n76
Wisd	4:	3	85
	8:	7	141n71
	17:	18	65, 133n44
Sir	13:	4	85
	17:	10	132n43
	22:	19	140n53
	33		4
	51:	12	132n43
Joel	2:	26	132n43
Zech	3:	2	140n56
	4:	7	141n76
Isa	1:	4	140n56
	14:	20	140n56
	42:	10	141n78
Bar	5		10

C. NEW TESTAMENT

Matt	9:	13	137n14
	12:	7	137n14
	14:	12	140n55
	22:	53	140n54
	23:	23	137n14
Mark	15:	45	140n55
1 Cor	12:	13	140n56
Titus	3:	5	137n14
Heb	14:	6	137n14

INDEX TO AUTHORS

Arndt, W.   132, 133, 134, 137, 138, 139, 140, 142
Baars, W.   10, 11, 117, 118, 120, 121, 122, 124, 133
Begrich, J.   10, 113, 121, 145
Blass, F.   130, 136, 137, 138, 139, 140, 141, 142
Browning, R.   139, 140
Charanis, P.   143
Colwell, E. C.   36, 123, 125, 126, 127, 130
Curzon, R.   143
Debrunner, A.   130, 136, 137, 138, 139, 140, 141, 142
de Jonge, M.   11, 120, 121, 122
de Lagarde, P.   7, 119
Denis, A.-M.   115, 118, 145
Dupont-Sommer, A.   115
Epp, E. J.   115, 126
Fabricius, J. A.   7, 119
Finegan, J.   131
Fritzsche, O. F.   7, 119
Funk, R.   133
Geiger, E. F.   7, 119
Gingrich, F. W.   132, 133, 134, 137, 138, 139, 140, 142
Gray, G. B.   10, 120, 121, 131
Hann, R. R.   11, 116, 121, 124
Harris, J. R.   6, 10, 118, 121
Hilgenfeld, A.   7, 119
Hort, F. J. A.   97, 110, 142, 143, 144
James, M. R.   7-8, 116, 118, 119, 120, 122, 132
Jellicoe, S.   100, 142, 145
Kraft, R.   145
Kuhn, K. G.   10, 121
Kuhn, T.   100
Martin, R. A.   138, 139
McReynolds, P. R.   2, 36-38, 39, 40, 55, 126, 127, 128, 130
Metzger, B. M.   38, 39, 101, 110, 123, 125, 127, 131, 132, 134, 138, 139, 140, 142, 143, 144
Milligan, G.   80, 138
Mingana, A.   10, 118, 121
Moulton, J. H.   80, 138
Nestle, E.   123
Pesch, W.   10, 121
Pick, B.   7, 119
Purintun, A. E.   145
Rahlfs, A.   2, 3, 5, 11, 12, 13, 14, 38, 115, 116, 117, 118, 122, 123, 127, 128
Robertson, A. T.   130, 131, 132, 137, 140
Rost, L.   115, 145
Ryle, H. E.   7-8, 116, 118, 119, 120, 122, 132
Sandmel, S.   115
Swete, H. B.   8, 9, 10, 11, 120, 121, 122, 132
Thackeray, H. St.J.   136, 137, 138, 139, 140, 141, 142, 143
van Groningen, B. A.   135
Viteau, J.   6, 10, 118, 119, 121, 139
von Gebhardt, O.   3, 5, 7, 8-10, 11, 12, 13, 14, 35-36, 39, 40, 49, 50, 53, 62, 68, 69, 97-101, 102, 104, 116, 117, 118, 120, 121, 122, 123, 124, 125, 128, 132, 133, 134, 135, 137, 139, 142

Wellhausen, J.   7, 119
Westcott, B. F.   97, 110, 142, 143, 144
Wisse, F.   2, 36-38, 40, 49, 126, 127
Wright, R. B.   11, 13, 14, 115, 116, 121, 123, 124
Zahn, T.   118
Ziegler, J.   3, 116, 117, 121, 128, 129, 145

www.ingramcontent.com/pod-product-compliance
Lightning Source LLC
Chambersburg PA
CBHW021144230426
43667CB00005B/241